WHERE LOST IS FOUND

NAVIGATING SEASONS OF CHANGE WITH SNAKES, GRACE, AND A DIVINE DOG

STACI MCCORMACK

Library of Congress Control Number: 2025903384

Paperback ISBN: 978-1-966283-34-8
Hardcover ISBN: 978-1-966283-35-5

    1. Main category— Nonfiction > Biographies & Memoirs > Memoirs
    2. Other category—Nonfiction › Self-Help › Motivational
    3. Other category—Nonfiction › Self-Help › Personal Transformation

Published by: AR PRESS
Roger L. Brooks, Publisher
roger@americanrealpublishing.com
americanrealpublishing.com

Table of Contents

Before Step #1

Prepare to Move from Incubation Period

THIS IS A STORY ABOUT dimes, a boy-turned-man, an otherworldly presence on the front porch, and light slipping into a place and space that was feeling a little gloomy-ish. Oh, and snakes too. Yes. Snakes.

Careful. There are some scary concepts in this book. Concepts such as a serpent infestation in the dwelling I call home, teenagers, perimenopause, way making, career angst, and a gnawing intuitive calling to start evolving my life and my place in it. Perhaps the scariest concept of all? Confronting life-season transition without much know-how.

This series of real stories that breathed air into my deflated spirit, while cradling my authentic self when I needed it so desperately, are just that—real. Real son. Real dog. Real snakes. Real.

One holiday, some time ago, I found myself standing in the middle of my living room among disenchantment, lack of enthusiasm, grief, hesitation, longingness, a dimmed light, and snakes. I saw the words sprinkled upon my then-tired life script, and there I embraced my current reality. My life was shifting before my very eyes.

In that living room, in that moment, I gazed upon my hormonal teenager and saw my ridiculously overwhelming list of to-dos for work. I met the most foul snake kind of scent emanating from the lower level of our home, and I glanced at a Christmas tree that lacked holiday cheer. Right then, I realized that the need to rattle every single thing about the way I thought, parented, navigated my profession, and planned for tomorrow was more than just something to consider. The brutal truth was starting to surface: evolve or remain stagnant, crusty, and unsettled.

I determined the old way of grieving the loss of long-past moments of momhood to a little boy was exhausting. The old way of running, striving, struggling, and searching within my career was a suck-hog draining my energy, joy, and life force daily. The old way of standing down from stagnation would no longer take hostage of my creative, rock star, amazing self. A quiet voice from within was calling me to consider considering new ways of walking through each day. Time to begin crafting a revised daily walk. Time to return to the girl within the woman. But how?

These real stories about dimes and a boy-turned-man, an otherworldly presence, and light slipping into a place and space that was feeling a little gloomy-ish…oh, and snakes too, yes, snakes? These stories have now become my way-maker navigation tool; my set of directions for personal evolution, my step-by-step guide to transcend me beyond the encroaching angst and melancholy that surfaces when one season of my life has ended and a new one is on the horizon. It is my hope these steps, these giggles, this dog breath, these tears, and these broken snakeskins within these pages inspire you to evolve as well.

These rather simple transcend-through-cosmic-life-seasons-with-ease directional steps surfaced from the soul of a way-maker pup. And now, these steps are mine only because I lived among them and was inspired by them. The real credit for developing this life-transition roadmap is Jesus, who came to live with us in the form of a dog.

After now having surfaced out of the muck of old-way thinking, I, of course, have glorious hindsight. I see that our human lives mirror the cyclical cycles of Miss Nature's life. We are seasonal too. Without this foundational knowingness deep within our core, we miss the wisdom-messages that arrive in sanctuary moments. I understand my recent evolution was a result of my faith in myself and my knowingness of from where I come. Personal transcendence came from quiet, private moments with the four-legged being who arrived incognito. It came from permission I granted myself to accept my role in this place called Earth. It came from predators and breaking the necks of resentment, toxicity, regret, and the clinging to ways of old. It came in recognition of the power of ebb and flow and the falling apart and coming back together.

Befriending the need to move from an incubation period to actually crafting my new season of life was the first step in becoming a part of the natural order of things. Willingness to take charge of my growth and expansion came from gut-wrenching, never-goes-away-only-shifts grief. Reconstruction arrived from soaking up tiny moments of purposeful awe-finding in each day's walk. This thing named Evolutionary Spirit came from lying upon worn rugs in holy spaces. It came without words. My ability to navigate my way through one of my most difficult transitions came from employing strategic behaviors that were, in hindsight, the dog's way of navigating through life's speed bumps. You will find that this canine's intentional roadmap was inspired by a calling so deep within her, it came only from a higher power.

It takes guts to wallow for a bit in the grief life transition can bring. It takes guts to pause long enough to accept old ways are just that—old. It takes guts to recognize that sometimes just sustaining our life is not thriving. We are here to flourish amid every season and every metamorphic process. We are here to soak up the sunshine, to follow our call, to protect our mind, body, and spirit from predators and to answer the damn door (that's Step #7). Go on now, grab the leash. Dive into your first evolutionary step.

Oh, and if you don't know Jesus or are even a bit new to this Jesus story, no matter. I am forever learning about and exploring the unfathomable story of the man who walked here once. After all, I'm just a girl in a grownup body. I know you love dogs. And that alone is enough to start your own way making for your personal transformation.

Step #1

Watch for the New Thing

IT's PROBABLY NOT APPROPRIATE OR wise or politically correct or profound or attractive to say that one time, a bit of Jesus came to live with my teenager in our home in the form of a dog. So I won't say it. But…a dog, with many names and an otherworldly energy, once entered my life story as a new family member in my snake-infested home. Just in time. Right? Snakes.

If you're even a teeny bit like me, you identify as being one who appreciates animals, domesticated or not. I mean, who among us can look eye to eye with an ancient turtle without being transported to another place and time on this earth? Who hasn't looked into a cow's eyes and felt the soul rumble within? Maybe you. Maybe not you. Maybe you haven't be-friended a turtle or a cow but you have, in one season of your life, found a bit of profound love from a cat or dog or chicken or a pig named Wilbur. If you're that person, you will believe these stories. You know, as I came to know, that even in the midst of crazy life-transitions, it is very possible we are gifted a paw, a wing, or a hand to hold. A connection that offers hope, light, life-giving nutrients, it's-gonna-be-okay vibes, and grace. And, dare I say, all of that could come in the form of Jesus dressed like a d-o-g?

Many moons and oh so many days ago, a couple deposited a new thing, an indescribable, unexpected new thing. A puppy was lovingly delivered to our home's front stoop where the teenager lived. And so it was. A few storybook mini-me-memoirs surfaced within my big, little life.

These tiny stories surfaced inside of my unrecognizable wandering self. The main character in these pages entered in the aftermath of the death of my mom and during a palpable shift in relationship with my child as he began his own transcendence to adolescence. The other Heaven-like characters you will come to love arrived during my endless days of swimming through insurmountable loss of ideas and people, limited thinking, crushing pressure from work, endless projects and shifting relationships with everyone from family members to grocery store employees, worry about every little thing, and from the not-so-quiet messages I was choosing to ignore that were gently pushing me to consider my next life season.

The characters in this life story of mine arrived as old and young. They came on two legs and even four. Some flew through as a gentle breeze and others stayed. Well, one in particular stayed. The four-legged one. And the writing of these stories was influenced by nothing but angelic dog spirit in so many forms. This series of life narratives made of oh so many words I now call "my way-maker story." They were intimately shaped, and, you may find, some have a bit of leftover snakeskin hanging upon them. But that piece of these stories is just the leftover trauma part. More later.

Where Lost is Found

Isaiah 43:19 (AV)

See, I am doing a new thing! Now it springs up; do you not perceive it? I am making a way in the wilderness and streams in the wasteland.

Step #2

Intentionally Pack That Backpack

B EFORE THIS SERIES OF TINY memoirs unfolded, I did not know then what I know now. Wandering, operating on autopilot, settling instead of designing the daily walk, and simply existing are desert ways. Surrounding myself with myself, healing the soul, and waking each day with an evolutionary mindset are ways of empowerment.

Before I wrote these words, my foundational values, my run-strive-struggle-search mode, and my daydreams of cozy mountain-top cabins, perfect roaring fires, and Thanksgiving gatherings were beginning to come unglued in the heart of my midlife angst. Before these stories, I did not realize I was in the wilderness, wandering and lost without my evolutionary tools in my backpack.

Because I have been given the gift of living on this planet for decades, I now have hindsight and can use the phrasing "before (fill in the blank)" or "after (fill in the blank)." This language grounds me when I am thinking or speaking of my past, present, and future. You know this language. You do. There's before COVID, after COVID, before Christ, after

Christ arrived, before sliced bread, after sliced bread, and before menopause, after menopause. Okay, maybe that one is not too familiar to you. Finally, there is before tiny memoirs unfolded, after tiny memoirs unfolded.

BTM (before tiny memoirs), I carried a backpack daily. It was enormous, made all kinds of jingly noises as I plodded through my daily walk, and was, I must admit, super stinkin' impressive. In it was Gorilla Glue that kept me planted in one spot in my life's story. Magic potions helped me cling to just one more day in this job I had outgrown. Fairy wands were readily available to wisk-wisk over my child so I could continue to see him as a little boy and therefore could parent him the same way I had for years. Erasers were kept in the outside pocket to eliminate grief. A blindfold was at the ready to block out the obvious shifts occurring in all of my relationships. Parent tapes were kept in the side pockets, and I played them often in my head. Tapes that reminded me that girls are secretaries or moms or teachers only, and if you're a real wild girl-child you could be a nurse or flight attendant. Tapes that reminded me if I didn't have a fancy title like, say, school principal, I was just a girl. Not influential. Not fancy. Just a girl. I also carried around fifteen to twenty-five pounds of worry and stress. Boy, carrying those pounds around got to be a sweaty undertaking when I entered the perimenopause phase. In the backpack were lots and lots of recycled grocery sacks and coupons that would save me a dime, my list of projects to complete, and 7,401 sticky notes to help me remember the things that I was to remember. One time at work, while sitting around a conference table, I pulled from the innards of my backpack an entire cucumber. True. I explained the cucumber was today's lunch plan. BTM, I carried agendas, pictures of me and my sister when we were little, toxic self-talk, and a very dilapidated worn map. The life rut I was in made a hole right through the paper atlas.

ATM (after tiny memoirs), I carry a much smaller pack and proudly wear that fanny pack on my, yep, fanny. Now, I carry around only my evolutionary tools. I carry sunrays, fallen leaves, pebbles, and heart rocks. I carry sweet nothing notes that, when spoken aloud, sound like, "I am perfect as is, I am influential, I do not walk alone, and I'm seen." I carry wildflowers strung together in a circle fashion. I now carry these things, ATM, because I also carry the knowingness that only the brave dare face the idea of personal evolution and life season head on. Oh! And now, I also carry a wickedly inspiring story about dimes and a boy-turned-man, an otherworldly presence, and light entering into a space that was feeling a little gloomy-ish. And snakes too. Yes. Snakes too.

Psalm 107:4 (AMPC)
Some wandered in the wilderness
in a solitary desert...

Step #3

Listen to Marge, Let Go of the Dime

SOMETIMES, IT'S NOT A BOOK or a far-out meditation session that brings life-altering messages or clear directions for our path. A new perspective can come during an unexpected encounter with a couple or group of friends, and sometimes it can come from one simple, quiet, single human being.

You know how people or places are presented upon your life path at just the right time? They may stay for a day, a year, a season, or just a moment. You do know this. You do.

On a rare occasion, a person named Marjorie, who works at the local market in the self-checkout lane, sees her schedule hanging in the break room one day. It states she is to work on the same day I shop at the local market. And, so, into my story enters Marjorie.

On this one particular grocery day, I found myself struggling to make the self-checkout machine stop demanding me to bag my item before proceeding. "Bag your item before continuing, bag your item to continue," it droned while I attempted to get my stupid ten-cents coupon to register as such on the electronic receipt.

I became irate, and a fight between me and the register ensued. I had, after all, taken the time to cut the dang coupon out of the Sunday paper and place it ever so gently in my wallet. After several attempts to scan the bar code across the register's black window that had previously been made gooey with the juice of an overripe avocado, I felt my blood rushing into my neck and brain at an uncomfortably fast pace.

During the sixth or seventh attempt, I thought, *I know what I'll do with this ten-cents coupon. I'll shove it up inside this machine so far that its robot voice won't be able to speak, let alone publicly shame me.* Before my head blew off my neck, I gasped in a cleansing breath and felt my eyeballs rolling wildly under my closed lids.

Just under my exhale, I heard a voice within. *Where did all the workers go? Who sat at the conference table to decide that all shoppers should memorize produce PLU numbers and bag their own stuff and scan their own stinkin' ten-cents allergy medicine coupons? Who was it?*

With little balls of perspiration peeking out of every pore on my nose, I semi-erratically shook my head to the right and the left, back and forth.

"Where? When? How?" I mumbled with spittle escaping my lips.

At this very moment in the universe, my rolling eyes caught a glimpse of Marjorie. She sauntered up to my chaotic self-checkout mayhem with her nametag prominently displayed upon her corporate apron.

"You got that?"

I turned my now sweaty face, my crumpled and fisted stupid stinkin' coupon, my disheveled bangs, and my Barbie-fake smile toward Marjorie.

"Well, Marge. May I call you Marge? No, Marge, I don't. I run an organization of sorts, Marge, and I am responsible for a million-plus dollar work budget. I raised a kid and a turtle, a chicken and a fish. I suffered the loss of my parents, friends, and relatives, and I have suffered the loss of my dream of impacting the world but, no, Marge. I don't. I. Don't. Have. This."

Then Marjorie sort of chicken-necks my self-righteous being and simply replies, "Sometimes, girl, the price it costs to save a dime ain't worth the toll it plays on your soul."

And just like that I find myself standing in the self-check-out lane with a coupon in my hand, my fruit bagged up in the recycled sack I brought from home, and tears in my eyes. I was on the path less traveled and was navigating without a map. I was lost and not found.

The profound metaphoric statement from Marge altered a tiny bit of my universe in just one blink of an eye and from that day forward. A dime? Beyond this sweaty coupon, could my dime be my grip on that toxic friendship or all of the crappy knick-knacks from one dead aunt's home? Was the dime that resentment, that hurtful word from my boss, or all of the melancholy related to my potential future roles as professional, parent, woman, and citizen? Was the dime the list I began to carry of how many times I spoke lately and found my voice falling flat upon the dinner table or the conference table? Was wandering upon a life path made of prior seasons I had already lived the dime? Was the wallowing in bygone days the dime I had pocketed when, in fact, some kind of new way was waiting?

Holding on to that dime does, indeed, take an emotional toll, Marge. Holding on to every dime means I'm not purging as I walk along life's path. More dimes in the pocket means less pocket space for me to slip my hands into on a brisk stroll through the park. And sometimes, when life gets chilly and the daily walk turns shades of dark, it's comforting to slip my fingers into the deep holes within my jeans—a palm-to-warmth union that fills my soul with memories of past childhood handholding with gigantic fingers, palms, and warmth that led me through the overwhelming and scary hustle-bustle of Chicago's busy streets. Hands that guided me upon the creaky wooden planks on the perfect fishing pier. In those childhood moments when I rarely felt confident or safe in the big world, I was consumed with the need to know that I was literally standing right where I was supposed to be. My father's gigantic hands that contained all of our ancestor's palms spoke, "*You belong here, on this pier.*" And "*Here, on this street right here. Do not move. Right here.*"

More dimes mean less breath, less faith, and less sacred space for light to enter. A pocketful of dimes means more weight and more stench. More dimes mean less time to awaken to the beautiful simple truths in this world and in this life of mine. More dimes mean less time to know and less time to practice the principles of simplicity. Clanking around with a bag full of dimes gives me less space to freely walk in the knowingness that the power to make a life filled with faith, peace, and flexibility in times of transition is within. Less clinging to ways of old is the only way to design the new.

Standing in front of that self-checkout machine, I heard the child within me gently speak love to my now somewhat wandering woman self. She whispered, *"Personal evolution is a dance between your younger self and our dime-drenched adult self."* A dance? I stood a half inch taller and thought, *I can dance. I dance in the kitchen, I do! Oh! Holy smokes. Like, yeah. Like, I'm a dancer.*

My biscuit-sized, pudgy childhood hands have now become wrinkled and sun kissed, but I can still summon a pair of hands that guide. When I am not sure where to be or where to dance or stand, my child within can grab a spirit's hand and the woman can speak aloud, "Oh, here I am. Here I go. I'm safe right here. I'm here. I'm right where I need to be." A dance between the child that was and the woman who is. Holy moly. My child within is stinkin' smart. Sometimes, returning to the girl within the woman is the wisest, most supportive act of love we can grant ourselves.

I swayed these dancing thoughts from my mind and returned to survey Marge. Her gait and her soft crow's feet served as evidence that yes, Marge had to have released a few dimes from her past. Safe to say, she had indeed lived in the chaos life transitions and personal evolution can present. Marriage? Divorce? Not being seen? Bankruptcy? No sense of purpose? Loss? Empty nest? Adult children's incarceration? Illness? Loss of identity and calling? Addiction? Maybe. Probably.

She was still presenting as wise, beautifully weathered, capable, empathetic, strong, steady, and forgiving. She was throwing sacred moments and wisdom into her day and others' too, for Heaven's sake! She was intentional and present, not flashy and obnoxious. Amid her rocky evolutionary process of moving from being this person to that person, she must have allowed time to embrace herself.

She stood before me in her masterfully crafted, still very important life. She knew that the power to create a life filled with authenticity, faith, and connection to self comes in small moments during the daily walk. It comes in checkout lines, sitting with tea, and in the ordinary life moments called the in-between.

Oh, this Marge. She was a smarty pants. I knew she knew because stinkin' brilliant words don't come from folks' mouths who haven't done the work. Marge knew how to dance with her child within. That day, she'd followed the calling to wear that apron, because in that corporate uniform she was influencing my world simply by suggesting I let go of a dime. Move from this place to that. Move from this clipped-coupon clutching persona to a wild woman who forgets to clip. I heard a quiet, unsure voice in my soul encouraging me to move through. Move beyond. Move forward a bit less weighted. Release the dime. Yes, let go of the dime.

Who likes the smell of old money, anyway? Not me, Marge. Not me. And so it was. I had, with the help of Marge's wisdom, begun to open a space for new to enter.

Matthew 6:19 (AMPC)
Do not gather and heap up and store up
for yourselves treasures on earth.

Step #4

Embrace the "With"

I SEE THOSE THAT CAME AND went. When I am open, present, and willing to entertain the wildness of this universe and this very community we call Earth, I am able to see before me and behind me. I see above me and below me. I see my ancestor in the beginning of creation huddling in the storms and dancing in the sun. I see my forefathers and foremothers being a part of the creation of nations. I see them crossing waters in search of safety, freedom, and promised land. I see them hand weaving clothes and struggling and triumphing. I envision them looking at their reflection in the water and, in their reflection, they see me behind them. Within the wrinkles of their faces are reflections of future me. In those ripples are me and the girl I was to become. I see my ancestors watching Father Sky and Mother Earth birthing dreams and seeping hope into each one of their children's steps. The very DNA of their traumas and triumphs is deep within mine. I see them, and they are the link to all I am.

They are not here, no. And I was not there. But, through the energy of soulful connection to their almighty and the deep knowingness that this story I walk today is not just about me, I can be with. With. I was with them before I was here, and they with me before I leave.

It's when my head swivels backwards, I see my angels. They arrived way before my days of professional stress and parenting woes. Way before snakes and birthday cakes with forty-plus candles. They arrived without wings visible to the human eye. They were incognito and were with me then. With me. Today, when I look back upon my childhood, my teen years, and even my early adult years, I see I was never truly alone. Perhaps you too hold close to your heart a story from your earlier days where an angel's hand appeared unexpectedly. To this day, I remember me as a young twenty-four-year-old girl in a hoopty car with a flat tire on a Wisconsin highway. My angel-man pulled up beside my naïve self and changed my tire for me in the frigid Wisconsin tundra winds. He may have figuratively and literally saved my life.

As I pen this thought, I also remember the young couple who entered and graced my midlife, angsty, stuck-in-a-rut, hot-flashy sweaty fortysomething life in a profound way, right smack-dab in the middle of my foggy evolutionary life transition with a simple knock on the door. Angels in incognito? Here? Now? Where do I stand?

1 Kings 8:57 (NLT)
May the Lord our God be with us as he was with our ancestors; may he never leave us or abandon us.

Step #5

Craft a New Script

As I stand with hindsight in my back pocket, I see the brutal truth. During that teary self-checkout line day, I see I was not certain who I had become. I had misplaced the little girl who was creative and tied dandelions into necklaces under shade trees. I could not recall the last time I painted a rock or laughed with tears running down my cheeks. I had been playing so many demanding roles in a production called *Life*, I lost the script that had my authentic self in the title. I had been clinging and clawing. I was running, striving, struggling, and searching.

Not having exited the self-checkout lane, I stood there stupefied. In this middle-aged season of my life, I felt lost in a desert. I was soulfully thirsty and desert burnt. Burnt out.

My dead aunt's face flew through my mind, and I remembered her posing a question to my child self, "What do you want to be when you grow up?"

"A poet," my ten-year-old-lips uttered.

"No, I mean a real job," she replied.

Mr. Randy, my college academic guidance counselor flew across my mind. In my self-check line daydream, he was advising me at the start of my junior year in college. I had not chosen my major field of study, and he insisted it was time. "Well, what do you want to do?" Mr. Randy asked, erratically tapping his pencil on his desk.

"I want to be a public speaker."

His eyes rolled. "Well, what would you ever talk about?"

Hmm, I thought, *that's a good question.* I told him that after I grow a bit more and finish college, I'll have a lot to talk about.

"You better just be a teacher because you're never going to make a living being a public speaker." With that, a schedule of classes was placed in my hand for my final two years of college.

Marge glanced at me and my dreamy eyes as I stood there with her in the checkout line. I ticked my head back and forth. Apparently, some of those dime-dreams were still deep within my heart. For so long, things had been happening around me while I stood in the middle of the production waiting for intermission. I was expertly playing the various roles of mom, partner, good neighbor, and professional. Like a well-rehearsed actress, I knew all the lines in each script for all the situations at home, at work, in the cul-de-sac, and at the weekend youth sports games. While operating in autopilot mode was sufficient and efficient, I sensed it was time to…let go of a dime?

I began to take notice that my words, my way of contributing, my influence, my leadership, and my mothering had shifted and had begun to lose impact. My external voice no longer matched my internal voice, and perhaps it was because I was using ways of old. The script was painfully boring, and

I knew the tired endings for every scene. There were so many signs pointing me to a new way of being in the world. My season was shifting, my memories were surfacing and inviting me to see. Intentionally, I had been ignoring these signs of change coming. I was ignoring the messaging. It was so easy to cling to that which I knew. But—yeah, but.

It's difficult to play the role of responsible daughter when your parents are dead. It's difficult to be the sweet mama who reads bedtime books to the little one who now wears Cheetos in their newly grown mustache. With back-pocket hindsight, I now know exactly where I stood in that self-checkout line. I had checked out. I had not recognized that I better get a giddy-up and start imagining a new place and an evolved state of being. Right then, right there, Marge's wisdom, her dime philosophy, and her empowered persona brought to my consciousness a new awareness. I knew not where to go. I knew not how to be my own warrior way maker. I knew not how to take the current me and mold her into an updated version of herself. But—what I did know, what I felt confident in professing, was that in this moment, I stood in the transition gap and was willing, yes indeed, to explore more about this thing called personal evolution.

Marge looked at me as if inviting me to take the first step on the path less traveled. "Hey, Marge," as I exited the self-checkout scene, "what aisle can I find cheap evolutionary tools?"

Hebrews 11:8 (AMPC)
By faith, Abraham, when he was called, obeyed and went forth to a place which he was destined to receive as an inheritance; and he went, although he did not know or trouble his mind about where he was to go.

Step #6

Free Yourself from Those Chains

THE EARTH DEPENDS UPON ME to stand as the tallest weathered tree in the forest one day. I must, for my own thriveability, become more than I was yesterday. More wise. More reflective. More selective. More present. More quiet. More me. It has been solidified again and again for me that inside of life's transitional stages is the constant presence of God. Yes, God, and sometimes leftover snakeskin.

Something bigger than ourselves is here. When we stop long enough to breathe in the miracle of the power of universal energy (yes, breathing—like breathing in a thing—a noun), we realize this power, these atoms that create us, nature, wind, and rain is what brings the delightfully unexpected storm. As real as my skin, my toes, my goosebumps, my cells, my heart, and my thoughts are. I am confident. I am assured in our life-season shifts—when the path is unclear, the purpose is foggy, and the daily walk feels unrelentingly foreign—is where the calm chaos lives. In the space of this tiny storm is also where grace, vibes, knocks on the door, and invitations to shift our perspectives lives. In this space, the new is invited and unexpected thrives.

Liberation comes when the dust of old is swept away. Driving away from Marge, I wiped the wet from my eyes and committed. I shall free myself from chains of old, have faith in rebirth, and move forward. Simple. Easy peasy. Right?

Isaiah 52:2 (NIV)
Shake off your dust; rise up, sit enthroned, Jerusalem.
Free yourself from the chains on your neck...

Step #7

Answer the Damn Door

As SURPRISED AS I WAS when the knock fell upon the door during the chill of one Colorado winter, so too were the apostles when Jesus knocked upon their hearts. The messy lot of disheveled future apostles turned their heads toward the knock and considered the ask Jesus posed to them. Could hanging out with Jesus and for real believing in His words bring light in dark, calm in storms, way-making in wandering, and mercy and grace in fallibility? They shook their heads with small doubting right and left tics.

When this particular chilly knock came upon my snow-dusted door, I instinctively ran into the kitchen and placed a dishtowel over my right shoulder like Mom used to do. The damp, stinky threads woven tightly together had soaked up spilled gravy and tomato juice drippings that had fallen down the side of the Ball canning jar. As gross as it may be, those woven threads were also occasionally used to wipe snot from little noses flitting about the house back in the day of my childhood.

My dishtowel shroud was thrown upon my chest and was now dripping down my back, caressing all my past trauma that had been caked upon my very being. In moments of facing the unexpected, I often reached for that which I knew. A dishtowel with a needle-pointed picture of a pumpkin sitting in a wagon sufficed for familiarity. Sometimes, the familiar comes in a bite of chocolate brownie or a low-carb, less-than-flavorful micro-brew. Just as Mom modeled for me decades ago, sometimes it's easier to escape the scene by masking the restless spirit in the midst of life's unknowns with a dishtowel.

This restless spirit struggled to envision who I was to become after dime purging. The struggle could have been a result of the undeveloped frontal lobe of my growing child and our shifting relationship. Perhaps restless spirit could have been the familiar dread felt when entering my workplace where the demands placed upon me as the building leader were impossible to meet daily. Where new initiatives from disconnected people drafting mandates at the state and federal level came far too often without additional resources to meet the new mandate. Where the only place children and teens are deposited on the front step each morning and parents place their trust that their child will thrive, be protected, and be loved all day. Where the darkness of our world enters through anxiety, mass shooting drills, peer isolation, unresolved mental health issues of students and staff, and often an unrecogniz-able aura of compassion fatigue blankets the brick-and-mortar building. Or, maybe, perhaps just maybe, this perimenopause restlessness was a result of the stench wafting up from the basement. This smell was something I was familiar with but had not begun to accept the fact that the smell was from the snakes. Squatters. Maybe I was restless due to the thing I was trying desperately to ignore. Ya think?

With dishtowel shroud draped, I danced a few shuffles to the knock upon the door. I stood in the entry way with Teenager and was draped in protective armor for the unknown.

I have lived long enough to know a knock on the door can move me into a frenetic search for the perfect hiding place, or it can bring me out of the forest where I am rummaging for random nuts of joy and promise. How the knock lands upon my heart is in the timing, my sense of readiness, my current sense of groundedness, and my ability to fathom and embrace the possibility of good.

The rat-a-tat-tat on the front door came again. And again. My holy night, silent night. Our vagus nerves jolted. Teenager glanced at me, and I silently nodded my head in permission to answer the beckon. This knock may have been bringing the promise of Santa or the Fuller Brush salesman, after all!

A palpable shift in the heart of the house occurred with each knock. Teenager flipped his dreadlocks off his shoulders in confidence, my eyes met Fit-And-Trim-Teenager's eyes, and he reached for the door handle.

I recall the dampness hanging in the air that day. The season of Christmas was present in decorations, yet the giddiness and anticipation seemed to have been absent. I looked upon the sparkling lights hanging upon the tree and thought, *How did I get here? How did I begin working seven-day, sixty-hour work weeks? How did my lacrosse and tennis playing son start getting bags under his eyes from lack of sleep, tears from breakups, too many secret parties? How? How did parenting go from hot chocolate bedtime chitty chats to missed assignments and unfathomable work demands? And how did the lamps no longer provide life-generating light? How did the dim come into this space without even knocking? How?*

Revelations 3:20 (NIV)

Here I am! I stand at the door and knock. If anyone hears my voice and opens the door, I will come in and eat with that person, and they with me.

Step #8

Be Aware of What You Attract

HE ARRIVED BEFORE. HE CAME before I noticed a dimming Christmas tree and a lack of holiday cheer in my son's countenance. His visit was prior to the knock on the unanswered door and before all my *How?* wonderings swimming about my head.

Truth was, I had been smelling them for months. Them. Them snakes. Before the expert was hired, I had seen them and sensed their presence in our home. I observed them sunning themselves in the front porch bush. To what extent the snakes inhabited our home I did not know. I had convinced myself that the few snakes I saw on the grass were most likely tourists and had no intent to stay. This assumption worked well for me. For a while. When the while was up, along with my anxiety, I phoned Snake Man.

Snake Man looked under our home's foundation. He grabbed his cell phone and made a quick call. With trembling hands and a voice just audible enough, I heard him whisper into his phone, "How can this many snakes be living here? *How?*"

In some circles, there exists a belief that there is a direct link between serpents and ick. This circle of friends might even suggest there is a strong correlation between snakes and horror or serpents and impending doom. Some humans make connection between serpents and Satan. Imagine. What I know? Snake pits, snake toys, water snakes, snake dreams: all the things of nightmares.

When snakes defend their nests, they emit a vile stench worse than month-old worn-by-a-teenager sock. I know this because, after all, Snake Man had schooled me, and I lived with multiple colonies of serpents. Within the colonies were a plethora of neighborhoods, and within each community was a highly functioning replication of human society. Under our home's foundation, I would come to learn from Snake Man, who I willingly hired to help at any cost, were snake neighborhoods where HOA fees afforded some of them more room to grow. "That's the neighborhood where the five-foot-long bullsnakes live," he said, pointing.

According to Snake Man, there were other communities under our basement foundation floor (and, according to Snake Man, maybe in the walls too) that must have had a wonderful school system, because hundreds of babies were present and thriving. Another neighborhood had the best of both worlds. They enjoyed a dark, cozy corner to huddle while they endured winter months and celebrated their three-exit access to easily escape my home when chasing the sun's rays each morning.

I followed Snake Man around the perimeter of the property while he sprayed a fine mist of what smelled just like dried oregano from 1992 I have stored in my cabinet today.

While he sprayed and strolled and sprayed again, the dialog continued.

We chatted about snake public schools, and I imagined snakes complaining about their HOA fees. My tongue wiggled erratically behind my teeth and my thoughts began to spin. *This is not good*, I thought. *Hosting colonies of snakes in our home rent-free is not the news I celebrate. This is not good n-e-w-s.* My insides churned as wildly as they do on the teacups at the county fair. Come on, Snake Man! Stop the ride!

Was what I emitted attracting anything but good news? In tandem with my stomach, my thoughts swirled and spun on this dangerous, cheesy teacup ride that I now shared with Snake Man. I placed my hand over my mouth to calm my nausea. Was my current somewhat negative energy and general angst oozing out of my pours and therefore attracting these snakes to slither their way into my home, my safe zone, my life?

Gas escaped my unsettled intestines and as the burp was released, the internal dialog continued. I knew taking personal responsibility to craft a daily walk after one season has ended and a new is beginning is the wisdom of a way maker. Intentional way makers listen to their voice within, allow grief to occur while saying good-bye to the way things were, plan, take calculated risks, explore, expand their thinking, and pack wisely. All these intentional steps make room for new light to enter. Paths of evolution and growth created in this manner are a result of intention, work, and manifestation!

The good-news gas allowed a harsh possibility to escape and brought calm to my intestines. Self-fulfilling prophecy can attract ick or possibility. Hey, perhaps this teacup ride was slowing, Snake Man. Just as I had planned my summer after high school graduation, I could now plan a new path away from snakes and all that comes with them. Now that, my friend, is very big good news.

Vigorously, I shook my head to make some sense out of this real-life drama I found myself living. The shake of the head was superbly effective in bringing my presence back to the moment at hand. Snake Man continued explaining the slithering, scaled, tongue-wagging situation. And just as old habits do, I found my mind surfacing some old, comfortable, yet not profitable, thinking long enough to explain to Snake Man that certainly these snakes did not choose to inhabit here in my home because they were attracted to the energy being released. No, I was certain. Not in our house.

As small and as sweet as puppy-breath utterings, these words surfaced within my heart: The law of attraction is simple, really. What we expend, we attract. And then with beady, glassy, black-pupiled eyes, I looked right into Snake Man's eyes and whispered, "How?"

The snake represents both spiritual danger, temptation, and deception in the Bible. Snakes also represent healing and salvation. Holy snake breath. If I had the guts back then when I stood among the creeping dim light in our home, maybe, just maybe...

No. No looking back on the creepy spiritual danger idea. This deep spiritual danger thought was not something I wanted to eat nor pray nor live upon smack dab in the middle of my home's snake infestation. Ain't nobody got time for deep thinking amid life-season transitional tsunamis such as midlife can bring. Or do we?

I learned three things I did not know before I hired Snake Man to rid our house of serpents after I watched Snake Man spray his fake-news, colossally ineffective snake-ridding oregano all over our home, property, and our basement. 1) Outdated oregano does not free a home from ick. It just ticks off the neighbors and gives everyone pasta nightmares. 2) This story of my snake-infested home and my learning how to intentionally navigate and create a new way to be in the world in a new life season is, miraculously, about healing, imagining, and salvation. 3) Evolution is about cooking with fresh, spicy ingredients and the purging of outdated spice. Transitions are about hard work, reflecting, and believing in an effort to make it so.

Snake Man and I never met again in that old Italian restaurant. I suppose he and several others in my life no longer added the spice my new life path craved. On the outside, Snake Man looked fresh, confident, and competent. But his oregano had gone stale. I am attempting to let go of things that no longer serve me, Marge. When I relied on Snake Man to solve all my snake problems, I was in the middle of practicing the practice of releasing others, dishtowels, shrouds, and expectations. I was attempting to release others who spoke of shallow living, snake things, and old seasonings. It was time. Time to shed relationships that bring only negativity, no hope, and drama. Time to effortlessly shed skin that no longer serves me. Easy peasy, right?

Should I call Snake Man for a few tips on shedding? Shall I inquire how snakes so effortlessly shed their skin each life season to allow room for growth? No. Our relationship is done. Over. I'm moving on. Finished. Done.

Proverbs 23:7 (KJV)
For as he thinketh in his heart, so is he.

Step #9

Befriend Your Truth

ONE TIME, OH SO LONG ago, there was a boy named Adam and a girl named Eve. They, according to the Bible, lived in a stunning place. There was free food, clean water, no cars, no punching in for the day's work, zero to no crime rate, beautiful nectar, and shade trees unlimited. A vacationer's dream was this place. Until the snake arrived.

This snake tempted both Adam and Eve to eat the fruit from the Tree of Knowledge that they were not supposed to eat from. I mean, gosh. What's with us humans? But they did. Yes. They did. The snake, who used its slinky tongue to whisper and entice Eve to eat the fruit, is considered in this Biblical story to be the creature in rebellion of God. The snake's goal was to lead humans to a death, of sorts. I wonder if Adam and Eve gave off a vibe of sorts that sent messages to creatures like sneaky snakes that the two of them were willing to entertain living outside of God's request to not eat from the tree. The consequence of eating the fruit against His request was free will, God had said. There would be no "you're grounded" or loss of driving privileges. The cause and effect was a simple science: apple eating equals free will. Stunning. And, really, that consequence doesn't sound too bad. Does it?

I imagine, in this paradise, Adam and Eve's craving for free will was powerful. Now, goodness. Isn't that so like the teen who craves free will. I imagine that fruit looked scrumptious. Maybe the snake picked up the we-are-vulnerable vibe Adam and Eve were dropping and, maybe, just maybe, what they emitted from their souls attracted what we now call a little bit of a mess.

That first book of Genesis in the Bible is unbelievably heavy. First there was the making of all creation in a miraculously short time span, and then there was the Tree Of Knowledge and the Tree Of Life and the garden scene. I find that whole fruit-eating scene to be a lot like peer pressure. We are given boundaries and yet are tempted still. But this story is not about peer pressure.

As the slinky snake watched Adam and Eve bite into that fruit, that clever serpent became witness to free will being given to all humans. Sounds exciting, doesn't it? Oh, it was. Until free will was married to human suffering that we still see play out today. It was many years after the fruit-eating scene when God sent Jesus to Earth. We were in a bit of a mess, after all, and God thought of no other way to love us and save us from ourselves than to send Jesus.

Jesus began to walk the Earth and began finding those that would carry his message after he left. Some of these men agreed to learn all about Jesus and his teachings. Now, in the beginning of Jesus's walk, these apostles were all just a bunch of regular dudes in transition. I imagine them looking around and feeling pressured to marry and get better jobs than being sketchy tax collectors or fishermen who didn't catch many fish. I imagine the pressure upon them to hurry and grow up was palpable. Their moms were most likely all over them like flies on honey. Even way back in the day, moms suffered the angst that comes from empty nesting and worrying about the child who is becoming the adult child.

These dudes, by the grace of God, dumped their jobs and decided to use their free will to follow this Jesus guy around as his apostles. In doing so, they believed this listening and learning walk with Jesus would help them to make a change in their own lives. Wow. Free will can be used to do new things, reinvent identities, and become a part of something bigger than oneself?

Jesus promised his rag-tag bunch of apostles that in the course of spreading the Good News they would be able to tread on serpents and scorpions. I didn't have apostles during my snake-infested home crisis or amid my midlife blahs. So, as I mentioned, I hired Snake Man to tread on my serpents. Snake Man who…well, we know how that turned out. Expired oregano and a sprayer thingy does not tread nor deter snakes from squatting in my home.

I was recently empowered through the acquiring of new knowledge. I have no-coupon-required free will. I reviewed what hired Snake Man had shared before our breakup. His words echoed in my head…colonies of snakes and the size, their preferred meals, and the skill they have to shimmy into any sized crack. Snake Man shared how cunning and agile snakes are. He pointed out the smallest of spaces near the home's foundation and explained, "These are the snakes entry ways that eventually lead them to the inside of your home."

I sat on my front porch after Snake Man had come and gone. With his words still lingering, I wondered if the snakes who were still living in my basement were the cousins or nephews and nieces of the snake in the Garden of Eden. I remembered the hope and promise I had clung to that hired Snake Man's magical oregano spray would rid my life-space of slithering ick. On that porch, I sat among remnants of his left-over, outdated spice still permeating the cushion of the chair I slouched into. I felt defeated and yet cautiously optimistic as I embraced the idea of free will and self-fulfilling prophecy.

I knew I was not yet accustomed to this much needed paradigm shift of intentionally crafting my next life season by using free will and packing my backpack with tools that inspire a positive life trajectory. Designing and way making as an older mom, an orphaned child after the death of both parents, and a professional seeking something more aligned to my authentic self was still a bit overwhelming. Facing my truths about my responsibility to care enough about myself to transform the friendship I had with myself was a bit big, I had to admit. The magnitude of the work I had in front of me to turn gloomy-ish into light, work into intentional play, unrealistic expectations into acceptance, and old spice into garden-fresh flavoring seemed a bit daunting, Snake Man. Transcending takes work!

Matching the frenetic energy of the birds' flitting about, I pounded my feet on the floor, working to disturb the morning routines of every one of those snakes below the floorboards I stomped. Looking down, past my feet, beyond the patio deck boards, I imagined life without snakes. I sang Ricky Dillard's "I'm Free." I stomped and jived and sang his soul-rocking, gut-popping, truth-speaking, "I am free!" I knew my truth. It would take a miracle to rid our residence of snakes, but I believed the miracle was coming. I believed it was almost here. Grabbing on to the arms of the rocker, I squeezed my hands around them a bit tighter and with each stomp I sang.

John 8:32 (NIV)
Then you will know the truth, and
the truth will set you free.

Step #10

Study Your Shift

RUSTRATION WITH MY TEENAGED SON'S recently developed deficits was growing. He had begun to resort more and more often to using deep-throated grunts to communicate. Low vibrations coming from the bottom of his throat escaped in response to my "How was your day?" and "Any homework tonight?" questions. This saying less and grunting more was a result of his increased testosterone coupled with his urge to create space between myself and his developing wings.

This new way of communicating with me was a missed signal that change was occurring in my world. My sighs grew heavier when reviewing my plethora of due dates for work. My eyes rolled further to the back of my head when realizing I missed sending birthday cards to those far away. My knee-socks stuck more to my shins with the impressive layer of hair I had grown. Those calves had not seen a razor in how long? All those miniscule messages, the eye rolling, the grunt frustration, and the hairy legs, were signs I had attempted to sweep under the rug. These small behavioral shifts were signs that indicated my world was changing, my priorities were shifting, and the way I ran the treadmill of life in my midlife season was not the way of my future. With hindsight in my back pocket, I now can sing Johnny Nash's song, "I Can See Clearly Now." The rain has gone.

I'm not an expert, clergy, or shaman. I'm a girl in a grown-up body. By the grace of many years on the planet, I have had the privilege and opportunity of years and years of growth. I never did the eat, pray, love thing as part of my evolution. However, I did eat hydrogenated oils until I started learning about aneurysms. Aneurysms may be ickier than snakes in the house.

One day, as I yoga-ed around my mat, I began to recognize that how my days unfolded in my twenties, thirties and forties were just a result. A result of what I believed about my own abilities, others, and the world. Basically, I started to see the stinkin' connection between what I believed and what actually came to be. Self-fulfilling prophecy.

What I ate and stress-prayed about and loved on was different in each decade of my teens, twenties, and early thirties. It all was also very earthly and, yes, somewhat shallow and, I guess, fine. For then. Until it wasn't. Until my treadmill forties, with snakes, increasingly stressful job demands, and Teenager's expressive language going from vocabulary to grunts, there was a gentle rising of awareness within. It blew a tiny voice encouraging me to pause, to study this shift that was encroaching upon my thriveability.

Transition messages come quietly, like the green leaf that changes to yellow. I promised myself that my future seasonal shifts will be recognized as the yellow in my green. Now it's my responsibility to embrace messages I am receiving. Embrace the language of the grunt. Embrace the new technology challenges at work and be braver than ever before to admit I no longer care to learn this technology. Embrace my response to angelic voices that direct where I need to stand. Time to embrace this unexpected nudge. I began to recognize the beauty in life's unexpected. I mean, who wants perfect? Perfectly shaved legs, a wildly less stress-filled job, a grunt-free teenager, or no snakes in my house. Unexpected for sure, but perhaps just what I need to propel me forward. Perfect is not conducive to necessary reflection that propels growth. I mean, who wants perfect, Marge? That's creepy, Marge.

I stood (still!) at the front door with Teenager. My world in the snake-infested home had already begun to transform. I stood in the aftermath of Marge's dime wisdom, Snake Man's expired oregano, and a new way of listening for signs of change. I realized the way I was currently living was a reflection of what I had already been doing for a very, very long time. This way of life was stagnation. Who I was then and the world I was living in now was simply not the same.

This knock at the front door presented as an invitation for me to become open. Open to being present with myself. Open to considering what is good. Open to utilizing this free-will idea while engaging more deeply in the simple act of appreciating ordinary life moments. Moments such as the wonderment surfacing again while watching a raindrop splatter on the ground, of watching how chocolate syrup caresses the scoop of vanilla ice cream melting in your bowl. Being-in-the-Be.

Being-in-the-Be: the simplest form of presence. Sitting inside of a no-agenda moment where no purpose is required.

A place where there is no martyrdom, no hurried, and no harried. No striving and nothing to prove is Being-in-the-Be. It is where I allow myself to claim my own enoughness and grant permission to surrender. Perhaps Being-in-the-Be is Heaven on Earth. It is free and resides in a wise soul's backpack. I promised more hot tea, more soaking up sunshine, and painting rocks to change my daily walk.

I folded my hands together and watched Teenager open the front door. In a voice as perfect as Cindy Lou Who asked grinchy Santy Clause, "Why are you taking our tree?" I asked myself, "Are you all in?"

Romans 12:2 (NIV)
Do not conform to the pattern of this world, but
be transformed by the renewing of your mind.

Step #11

Know This: Nature Brings Hot, Cold, Circles, and Puppies

I REMEMBER BEING BONE WEARY AS I stood tippy toes to see what Teenager saw before him. If meteorological elements speak, I am certain the atoms that made the weather on this day spoke. Each element was hanging in the in-between. A sweet, cool, sugar-coated breeze was present behind the blazing high-altitude sun. The breeze was not a wind and the sun was not the desert's. A symphony of birds chirped their song in the background and yet no large flock was seen. Precipitation from days past lingered just so in the air to make our skin ask for moisture but did not crave the likes of humidity. The yin and yang played magically together on this day. With the door ajar, I craved the balance that I lacked. I seemed to be incapable of intentionally adding enough yin to balance the yang. Or had I truly tried?

When nature speaks and we listen, we find the answers and the way. We see the cycles playing out as the seasons shift. We see tide roll in, linger for a moment, and recede, changed in form. We watch the tree shimmer in green, linger for a time, and purge in the fall, changed in form. Nature's cycles remind us how our lives are played out in circular motions. The circular way of things is the only way. Nothing ever really falls apart because with *apart* comes *together*. Cycles are love and loss, stagnation and growth. Striving and resting, questioning and discovering, lack and abundance are circle messages. Nature was inviting me to consider the in-between of cold and not, storm and calm, low tide and high. There it was. The in-between where, if we muster up the courage to take responsibility for our days and our lives and each moment within, we too are creatures who flourish, linger, change in new form. We can catch a sneak peek at the shifting clouds, watch them expand, flourish, linger, change form, and leave. I can cocoon, create, and emerge as a changed form. I relished in this awareness that I, too, was cyclical. I enter. I stay. Change. Leave. Enter, stay, change, leave in new form.

There they stood. There they were, the barely-old-enough-to-be-called-an-adult young woman and her spouse. This couple who stood stoically in front of Teenager was loosely tied to our cul-de-sac. On occasion, Teenager had served as lawn mower to the young woman's parents who lived next door.

On this day, in this moment, a bundle within Young Woman's arms twitched and showed a wrinkly belly and paws of gooshy goosh. Colors of black and white with pink underbrush invited kisses, with a tail as long as half of Teenager's thumb and teeth as white as arctic snow. The creature wiggled tiny squiggles. The couple and the Teenager spoke a secret language through vibrational string theory energy vibes and light source waves, and then Puppy opened her eyes and peered at Teenager through the heart-shaped black, wiry hair on her face.

Teenager held out his half-gallon hands in the shape of a bowl just big enough for a puppy. Filling a palm and a half, her presence was thus.

Was she and her four legs here to spread the Good News in the center of so much that seemed to be anything but?

Ecclesiastes 1:5–7 (NIV)

The sun rises and the sun sets, and hurries back to where it rises. The wind blows to the south and turns to the north; round and round it goes, ever returning on its course. All streams flow to the sea, yet the sea is never full. To the place the streams come from, there they return again.

Step #12

Consider Your Name

THERE'S SOMETHING ABOUT A NAME. I haven't had the colossal responsibility of naming only but a few creatures in my life. I name many things, including the plants in my world and the squirrels that frequent the front stoop looking for peanuts. Naming things helps me feel connected and grounds me upon the foundation of relationship. Addressing squirrels and trees by name is the sacred in many of my mornings. When watering Pretty, the plant, I speak to her and notice her growth, and we celebrate this moment of together. Robert drops by almost each morning to retrieve his peanuts-in-a-shell. As a squirrel, he needed his name to reflect his sensibility and the dry wit he displays when hiding behind the pole on the deck.

Beethoven, the tree in the yard, is a life-giver. She was a stick when she arrived, and I did not know what would become of the little twig. Her name comes after many days of watching her tremble in the ground as if she was moving to a silent tune. She came to me as a gift, and the presenter of the gift said he drove with her in his truck while listening to

Beethoven. Beethoven's music was within her very core and, just like the artist himself, people could not fathom that the boy would become a future legendary composer and pianist. The older I grow, the more immense and intimidating the task of naming becomes for me.

The first time Teenager played a lead role in a naming process was with his baby chicken. Kindergarten teacher Mrs. Johnson hatched eggs in the classroom. Talking about the entire incubation period with my baby son was the light during many dinner conversations. Then, kindergarten Five-Year-Old Boy taught us about the rigorous schedule required when playing surrogate mamma and explained that many supplies were needed to protect the fragile eggs: an aquarium "just this big" was necessary so everyone could stick their head through the top opening to peer upon the eggs, a lightbulb stuck into a socket that comes with a cord, soft grass from the recess playground for a bed until Mrs. Johnson replaces it with hay, and finally, sometimes these eggs needed a water bottle from a kindergarten backpack with a side of leftover Fritos from class-time snack break. "You know," Five-Year-Old Boy explained, "just in the event the chicks hatch during the night-time and are thirsty and hungry."

On the day the chicks hatched, Five-Year-Old Boy jogged quickly to the railroad crossing, stopped, looked both ways, re-adjusted the backpack and rocks in pockets, ran up the gravel incline, crossed the train tracks, and stepped onto our cement porch stoop. He appeared at our front door, where I'd had one ear upon the step waiting for his arrival and one ear inside the house. He presented his convincing request. "Mrs. Johnson said if we go to school after this I say and get to school so fast,

I can have a baby chick because, Mamma, the babies came out today in their egg they came out." And just like anything in life that ends up being a pure-bliss core memory, it was naïve spontaneity that led the way.

It was simple. The babies came out today and an adoption was in order. Out the front door, across the tracks, down the gravel incline, to the front door of the schoolhouse and Mrs. Johnson's classroom door we scooted. Five-Year-Old Boy gently selected and picked up his chick with two, half-cup hands. Cradling baby, backpack bouncing on his shoulders, curls on head reflecting sunlight, he walked up over the tracks with me in tow. Gingerly, he strolled the remaining parts of the gravel path and entered the house, escaped to his room, and fell asleep with the baby chick upon his neck. When he woke, proud Five-Year-Old Boy announced her name to be (drum roll, please) Baby Snuggles. And so it was written.

Those that have been named after their elders or ancestors actually adopt characteristics of them. I call this an author truth and naming a baby after someone is a noble way to honor the elder. My boy, named after an elder I never met on Earth who traveled the world, collected coins, and lived in different cultures is so present within my son's soul. My idea of traveling was a summer road trip to the Midwest to see family. Occasionally, the family packed up and camped in a nearby state park or off-grid spot. My son? An international backpacker. After a taste of college, he explored and discovered the beauty in others across our globe, tasted new foods, experienced traditions, saw sunsets and sunrises on the Pacific Ocean, and soaked in the beauty of paddy rice fields. While sleeping in hostels and cars and picking apples in the island country of New Zealand to pay for the next leg of the journey, love was found under a star-filled sky in foreign lands. Love. Real love.

As parents, we watch our babies as they grow, and we play the game of "when they grow up I'll bet they will be…" until the game gets turned upside down. We then may find the baby doing and being and living and expressing their ancestral, authentic-DNA, God-driven life all on their own. If and when we are brave, we step back and admit the authentic soul that emerged is so much better than what we could have fathomed. We realize their name became a part of their identity. If we are not careful in the naming process, a human has to walk around for years renaming themselves to match the calling from within.

Sometimes, our angel or God or Source surprises us by camouflaging as a Marge or a tire changer man or a puppy. As God is my witness, Couple watched my son roll the puppy from his half-gallon hands into his being. He held the wriggling creature in a cradle fashion mocking the shape of—dare I say?—a bed of hay, and whispered, "Come Here You." Come. Here. You.

Psalm 68:17 (NIV)
The chariots of God are tens of thou-
sands and thousands of thousands…

Step #13

Confront Your Predator

LIBBY DIED AFTER TRAUMATIZED VESSELS in her brain suddenly burst in her seventy-first year of life. And life she lived. As pure as the olive oil in the cupboard was my mom Libby. She radiated joy in the aftermath of thirty-seven shock treatments while suffering from what we now know to be postpartum depression in the dark ages of the late 1950s. Thirty-seven old-fashioned, 1950s shock treatments will do a real bang-up job of ridding oneself of postpartum depression. Additionally, thirty-seven zingers will rid a person of bits of their short- and long-term memory, their executive functioning, and the luster and sparkle in a new mom's hair color.

When Libby had teeth in her mouth, she used them to perform a renaming ceremony after we children engaged in shenanigans, such as living room lamp-breaking. She flapped her false teeth at my sister and me while wrapping her petite hands around our tiny seven- and eleven-year-old biceps.

Before her words of redirection came our way, her slow, now vice-like grip with petite, perfectly home-manicured nails began to squeeze our upper arms just a little and then a little tighter again. With each squeeze, she whispered between her pursed lips and locked jaw, "You girls were told to stop, and now look what has happened to the lamp."

Her teeth acted as gatekeeper for potential audible huffs and puffs of disappointment. Her teeth held back forbidden bad words like "golly" and "gee" while escorting us to separate corners in the room. We braced ourselves for what we knew was coming.

"Girls. Your name is Mud."

There. It happened. Just like that. After all those years, we were simply re-named. Just as the final word from a poet's pen drops upon the earth and leaves ripples upon our heart, there it was. Mud. Life forever changed. Our identities shed in one long discarded skin from our lamp-breaking, mayhem selves. Thoughts immediately began to race within our little brains: As sisters, how will we introduce ourselves with the same name? Is it one D or two? My name is Mud. Sisters looked at each other from their respective corners and mouthed the word, MUD. Within the confines of our corners, we exchanged glances, we flapped our arms while mouthing the new MUD names. We shook and gyrated and swiveled our hips while flipping our hair from one side to the other. We pointed to our chests and held our imaginary microphones while we lip-synched M-U-D. Muds just gotta be Muds. We attempted to fulfill our new identity without shame but, rather, honor.

Libby faced her adversity of shock treatments while wearing a full-on cuckoo's nest straight jacket. She suffered the looks from church parishioners as they secretly questioned their minister's wife's persona. Like me, you, and Come Here You, she made a few mistakes in her daily walk and suffered while wandering between this stage of life and that one. She knew too well what it felt like to go from health to illness, to the promise of new to a crisis situation. Only because of her resiliency superpowers and years of intentional work could she go from shame to self-determination. Her seasons were filled with many hot-to-colds and young-to-not-so-young. And, in the gap of this-to-that, she spent much time swimming in the transitional stage. These in-between transitions of hers were not unlike what I was experiencing in the very moment of puppy's arrival.

I recall a memory of mine that took place on one beautiful Sunday morning when the church congregation gathered after service. All sinners stood sipping tin-kettle coffee together in the fellowship hall. The two Muds were bopping into each other in the wide-opened tiled space like helium balloons blowing in the wind. Tears of laughter ran down the Muds' cheeks, and without warning, Libby raised her Styrofoam cup in the air, opened her mouth, and past her lips through her teeth came a piercing, "Girls! Stop acting like imbeciles!"

Now, us little Mud girls lacked the expressive language at such a young age to say something back like, "Um, like, Mom, maybe preachers' wives for some reason shouldn't be saying that." So we didn't. But in the crevices of our internal behavior meters, we knew our outrageous silliness was wildly inappropriate and probably worth the wrath it brought.

Sister and I knew Libby's executive functioning frontal lobe filter had been impacted during the treatments. Yet in moments like these, where things were said that maybe shouldn't have been spoken, memories were made. This particular memory is still one of my most favorites of Libby, the three of us, and my childhood life.

She had said aloud what every adult church-going parishioner was thinking. As inappropriate, unwise, stunning, and unattractive her redirection and highly offensive word choice was, Libby spoke her truth. She let slip from her forever-healing, fried brain a thought many of the parishioners wish they could have said. Having no filter was the making of tears-down-our-face-belly-ache laughter that lives on into infinity in my heart. No filter. All the time. All. The. Time.

When the helium balloon Muds were bopping around in that fellowship hall on that beautiful Sunday, Libby had reached her limit. Her savior instinct simply took complete command of the situation with the resources she had. From the outside, if one were to witness this scene play out without background knowledge, one would not realize that what Libby had to do in that moment was to protect. There were predators in that fellowship hall and in Libby's life.

Ridiculous behavior from her children, mean words, gossip, and unexpected panic attacks of her past trauma displayed in the middle of bible study and sometimes even choir rehearsal were her predators. Their prey? Her and her family's safety. Potentially, all of those elements could create havoc on the family, our reputations, and our good name, and they could uproot a professional from his bread-winning job.

Wise earth-walkers know predators can appear in the form of self-loathing, fear, loneliness, unresolved issues, or two little girls acting all-a-fool at church. Better yet, acting like Mud. Sometimes, when cats and pigs and dogs and humans do things, it comes from a place and space within, as if from some deep cellar within our soul. This place within me is where my unleashed predator protection instinct lives.

I mean, who hasn't been there? Called to act, called to protect, called to reach, called to text knowing that what might come out may sound a little harsh. Sometimes, the brutal truth is harsh. When onlookers take the time to understand where that behavior is potentially stemming from, we can gift a bit of mercy and forgiveness upon the situation and ourselves. Marge did this for me. So does Jesus. Every. Single. Day.

When Libby suffered what else but a brain aneurysm, she left the teeth she used to help tighten her jaw shut in our renaming ceremonies on the nightstand of her ICU hospital bed. Libby met Jesus without her teeth.

Before she passed, we placed a hoodie sweatshirt with prominent letters on it upon her chest. The S in the word Superman was capitalized. She was everything that S embodied. The warrior protecting us from monsters like what she'd suffered in receiving thirty-seven shock treatments. Libby knew what her past trauma was. She knew her trauma so well she could name it. And name it she did: Thirty-Seven Shock Treatments. She could point to it and speak its name. Libby had an intimate relationship with her past challenges. She knew her predators.

Through Libby I learned it's only when I can point to the trauma, speak it, and name it that I will find the reason in some of my behaviors and belief systems I now carry. It is through Libby I learned only when I name my loss of simpler days Grief and only when I name the flow of the stress hormone named cortisol coursing through my veins Toxicity that I can face them. Now that they are named, I can befriend them and then, with a wave of my hand, bid them goodbye. It was through Libby I learned that once I knew what predators stood in my way of conceiving a new vision for my future I could look them straight in the eye and name them Old Ways. I learned from Libby I can put my galoshes on and plod through the muck transcendence and way making brings. I learned I can gift myself grace. I can. Grace is sanctuary. Oh, sweet, sweet sanctuary. My friend, you are going to embrace Step #14. Sanctuary: the grace and space to imagine the next phase in this thing I name Life.

But this is not a story about Libby or about considering the grace and forgiveness we give to others and should be intentionally seeking for ourselves. No. This is a story about Come Here You, dimes, a boy-turned-man, an otherworldly presence, and light into a space void of human evolution while also feeling a little gloomy-ish. Oh! And snakes too.

Colossians 2:8 (VOICE)
Make sure no predator makes you his prey through some misleading philosophy and empty deception based on traditions fabricated by mere mortals.

Step #14

Create Sanctuary

THE FIRST GLANCE BETWEEN TEENAGER and Come Here You had occurred on the front stoop of our home. They laid eyes upon one another in the sacred space where the new was being birthed. From Couple's arms to Teenager's forever arms Come Here You was placed. Teenager's arms were now long and defined muscles complimented his newly chiseled chin—a far cry from his round little belly, poochy lips, and pudgy hands from Baby Snuggles days. Teenager shifted his mane of Bob Marley dreads away from his face and brought Come Here You into the same chest that cradled his deepened voice. As a new father, he protectively sheltered her meek, agile self into his arms. Gently, he placed her into his lap as he sunk into the ottoman.

Sometimes, during my daily walk, I find myself to be notably moved and keenly aware. Glancing at the two of them, I could feel my breath catch for a flutter of an angel's wings. Seeing my son supporting this baby puppy as if there was nothing more natural in the world caused me pause. In those moments of these, I embrace that within my very DNA are the stories of struggle, trauma, and triumph of my past family members' walks. I was reminded that I am birds' songs and dogs' whispers. I am morning mist's breath. I am day-moon and air flakes. I am part. I am Earth's blue aura. I am me. I am sparkle within puddle. I am one. I am one in this story.

In that moment of embrace between the two of them, Come Here You and Teenager personified fairy dust and warm evening dancing leaves. They blew hope and joy and baby breath into all that was to come. I did not recognize this moment to be the in-between or the Be-in-the-Be, and yet I stood right there in the sacred sanctuary moment where healing, re-creation, and evolution dwell. In sanctuary there is no need to battle. There is no martyrdom, no proving or plodding. In sanctuary there is no clutching or hoarding. There is no harried or hurried. There is only space. Sanctuary is where my presence is enough. A practice of creating the cause and condition for awareness wakening is sanctuary.

Teenager looked up with tear-filled eyes and uttered his eloquent, profound expression. "Ma, this all I need right now."

How does a shrouded dishtowel-wearing "Ma" respond to such a seemingly easy yet multi-layered statement from Teenager? What better way than in a thoughtful, strategic, confident, supportive manner?

I came to understand such big decisions needed time. In my earlier years, I was quick to respond and act. After a few regretful moments of saying things I should not have and doing things I wish I had not, I learned some ideas and decisions and choices need time to marinade. Giving myself time to think, to sleep on it, to breathe through a potentially huge commitment was part of me maturing into myself. Chewing

on thoughts and responses first were ways of intentional evolution. This act of self-care was a skill I would bring with me
in my next season.

Before responding to his request to make this puppy a
part of him, I slept and considered and chewed on the idea
of officially adopting Come Here You. A few days gave me
ample time to obsess over the oregano-scented herds of
snakes still residing in our home. I had ample time to have
a few more nightmares of snakes in the fridge and snakes in
my car. Between the not knowing how to rid my life story
of snakes and snake nightmares, I thought, *Do we not already
have enough animals living in our life story?* I needed more time
to ruminate, dream, and chew on these dog bone thoughts. I
needed sanctuary time more than ever before.

I stared at my son holding a cup and a half of promise.
"Oh yeah? Well, we'll see, won't we? After a few days."

Exodus 25:8 (NLT)
*Then have them make a sanctuary for
me, and I will dwell among them.*

Step #15

Welcome the Potential of a New Day

FOR THOSE "FEW DAYS" I walked. I strolled. I day-dreamt. I closed my eyes. I asked, "What would Marge do?" I moved about the few days with new awareness. I had grown leaps and bounds in the last few months. I had come to recognize the power in the potential of letting go, tossing the coupon, and releasing the dimes. Past seasons of handholding and recognition of ancestors as angels walking with me had opened my soul to exploring more of what this new season could bring. I found time to discard some of my expired spices and rolled my eyes at the ridiculousness in my expectation I placed on Snake Man to rid our house with just one spray can. I walked. I admitted my evolutionary backpack was still filled with dishtowels and snakeskins, but what I craved was something beyond. I was opening myself to the potential of good, to blessings I could not fathom. Blessings to drive my personal journey and blessings to evict the squatters in the basement.

When Jesus came to walk this Earth with real people who struggled with real problems in their real lives, he was intent to reach those that were marginalized and suffering. He delivered great compassion in tangible ways. For goodness sake, even his chosen and embraced apostles were an unconventional group of men. They were hormone-raging young bucks who were not previously void of engaging in sometimes sketchy behaviors—shenanigans, partying, and displaying boisterous, rowdy behavior. Jesus came to connect with all of us rag-tag humans.

If we are truth-bearing, we know we too have suffered, been afflicted, may have been or are still marginalized, and may have engaged in raucous behavior. We are that. All of us. In some fashion, at some point. When Jesus gave sight to the blind, caressed the leper, and healed the sick, he gained instant followers. He began sharing the Good News to all who would listen, and those with humble hearts were often the first to open to his messaging.

The poor, the meek, the lost, the wandering souls, the mourners, the addicted, the afflicted, the frightened, the alone, and the lonely were enveloped into his narrative, his arms, and his love. The common folk were inspired to rise, and their voices began to supersede the voices of those with positional power and wealth. The kings were too proud to consider his messaging. Perhaps they worried Jesus's popularity was putting at risk their own personal riches, power, and control. Jesus knew that when he went to the common folk they would embrace him, learn from him, eat with him. Those with less, those who were humble, those who were open, present, and willing were granted peace, healing, love, and a promise even inside of their in-between chaos. They were taught of forgiveness and redemption, and they were promised an inheritance of eternal life. Stunningly good news to hear that these truths are for us all, even after the Mud behaviors we may be guilty of.

His healings, his friendship, and his support to those who were outcast, ill, poor, lost, or lonely began to lead folks to believe that in his light and with his help they could cast out any lingering snake stench within their own lives. They could see things differently the more sermons they heard, the more miracles they witnessed, the more they grew in this thing called faith. It was as if Jesus brought a new day every day. In the midst of their own perimenopause, midlife blahs, and their sixty-hour-a-week toil, they began to conceive the potential of a new day.

After a few days of having puppy in our home, I returned to the kitchen with my towel still draped across my shoulders. I remember thinking, *Dishtowels in our lives are stupid.* Sometimes, they are renamed Mud when they hold us back from jumping into life and surrendering the old in the process of becoming new. Dishtowels keep us cowering behind the ways of old just like the ancient kings and pharaohs who missed Jesus's sermons because they couldn't bear imagining life any different than it was. When we refuse to consider to consider an awakening or a transformation of being, it becomes impossible for us to shed the old skin to become re-birthed again. Nasty wet dishtowels think they can cover and mask the issues for eternity, but the threads that are woven together to make this shroud upon my shoulders need a good washing. This dishtowel—do I even say it? It needs a baptism of sorts.

I remember thinking about potentially keeping the puppy, and I envisioned a scene from back in the day when Jesus walked. I saw the empty nester, the widow, the crabby employee, the weary parent, the recently divorced, and the bankrupt. There they were, huddled around a bonfire in the middle of a meadow on a cool evening. I myself was in that circle with the other afflicted souls. When I looked into the roaring flame among my friends, I suddenly had a sense of an unfamiliar spark igniting within, and I tasted this holy breath. I knew, staring into that light in my daydream, that simply being open was how I could become the light again in my own life. I could entertain new ways of sowing for my future self. I could hear the protector's footsteps surface within my daily walk. Was it perhaps time to see the light? The light in that bonfire certainly would keep those predators away.

The "few days" had come and gone. The time was now. I placed my dishtowel over the plastic rack in the kitchen, shook off its heavy presence, walked into the room where Teenager sat, and uttered eloquent words of support.

"Okay. You can keep her."

Just like that, I was in. I had opened my heart right there. I was now closer to a life free from dishtowel shrouds in a place where bonfires roared in a circle of others who were in the in-between but not alone. I felt the words tickle my teeth and fall into the space. We are blessed and so too are you, Come Here You. You are now us.

Matthew 5:5 (NIV)
Blessed are the meek, for they will inherit the earth.

Step #16

See the Miracle

AS SUNRISES AND SUNSETS WOVE themselves into the very bowels of the in-between gap of transcending from a boy to an adolescent and a young woman to an older mom, the vibrational energy of that original knock was still present within our home. It is difficult, if not impossible, to put a finger on the difference between before and after the knock. I was now keenly aware of the tiny moments in my life. Events such as eating cake at noon in the employee lounge and attending happy hour events to celebrate Wednesday or Thursday or Friday with not-so-close colleagues lowered my vibrational energy flow. Instead of cake-frosting buzz and cheap "Cheers," I began to intentionally pause before exiting my car to watch the raindrops fall, and I started to really deeply seriously read the mural painted on the wall of my new exercise class. *Me*, I thought, *in Pilates class! Dare I say?* Now, that right there was a miraculous shift. From the top of my lungs, I spoke in my car, "LISTEN! This day is not yesterday's, and tomorrow's day will require a new skill set and temperament and flexible approach. Give me an F, give me an L, an E, an X ability," I shouted to my massive imaginary audience I addressed on the imaginary stage I stood upon. Public speaking. Another dream that had not come true, Marge.

And so it was. Come Here You remained. Small events that I began to equate to small miracles started to occur. Now, wait a minute.

Is one miracle more profound or more valuable than another? Do some miracles require an extra-long queen-size mattress when others fit best into a twin? Jesus once turned nasty water into wine at a wedding to put the servants into the light while making the elite shudder in awe. You may have heard about that one. It was a really big deal. Is that miracle any less big than healing an afflicted person who suffered isolation due to a case of leprosy? I mean, how is the weight, impact, and value of an event or occurrence or a whisper in our head that tells us to travel a different road quantified? How do we not call a puppy potty training herself in a matter of mere days anything but a miracle?

After days of sleeping with Teenager in his bed, Come Here You began to learn the lay of the land. She confidently invited humans around a long, flat, furry, blue squeaky toy that looked as if it had been squashed by the tires of a Big Wheel. Someone had gifted the toy to the puppy and, in hindsight, as crazy as an Easter bunny being imaginary is, it resembled a run-over, carpeted blue snake.

Is this possible? A snake? I'm no statistician, yet the odds are insurmountably low that one friend chose and purchased a toy resembling a snake. Out of all the toys that could have been purchased for the puppy, this friend bought a snake? Come on statistician. This is just pure crazy.

The puppy used this blue snake to bring her boys to the carpet for a game of snake-and-drop. Among her boys, Come Here You would grab her toy snake, drop it, pick it up, and shake it violently. Grab, drop, pick up, shake. On the living room floor, Teenager and his friends gathered. All tables, ottomans, chairs, and other furniture that could have impeded the organic fellowship were removed. Instantly, as if gathered around a fire, the boys and their in-betweenness gathered. Come Here You led.

In humble postures, they played together as they communed. Come Here You had, just as Jesus had, collected them around a warm aura of a light, a new story, and a promise. The tone in this place we called home had begun to sing a slightly different note. Come Here You offered warmth and tenderness and whispered in Teenager's ear as they slept together, words of truth, "You're my boy. I love you. You are enough. You are already perfect. I am with you."

These play sessions with a flattened snake and a ball were small indeed, yet Teenager's face began to brighten. Miraculously, the light began to enter into cloudy spaces. As time progressed, Teenager began to find his way to the other side of angst. Peer relations, school, and athletic stress shifted. His bond with his new wirehaired BFF was a priority.

As much as I settled into Teenager's thirst for independence, I caught myself sensing a bit of melancholy as I recalled the earlier days when big kids were little, jobs were just forty hours a week, and there was always time to make chocolate chip cookies. As much as Dishtowel's ways were robotic and had been stunting my venturing into new territory of my woman-hood, I found it difficult to pause long enough to assess the current state of my own contentment. However, after placing that shroud over the dish rack days ago, something had shifted, and my desire to seek independence from used-to-be's was gnawing within me.

The brutal truth was starting to surface. Evolve or remain stagnant, crusty, and unsettled.

Opening, exploring, considering, transforming, evolving, and shaking the dust off were not the way of old. It was so much easier to hang on to the dime that was prioritizing work first and offering unsolicited advice to a teen who needed to find his own voice. These were days of a different place and time, a different season. These were ways of old. Not being able to recall who I am at my very core in moments of silence was the old. I found myself in the in-between and Come Here You stared right back.

Was the simple idea of considering to consider a miracle in itself? Setting personal boundaries among toxic humans were ways of new. Simply giving myself permission to walk away from the phone call, the lounge cake, the room where nothing is in there of value. Creating a new job for myself that was more aligned to my passions and skills but still within the same institution were ways of new. Simply imagining and playing with the possibility of a new job was empowering. Imaging myself ripping a piece of yellow, lined notebook paper that Dad left behind on Earth to draft not a sermon, but a list, was liberating. A list of my attributes and my leadership skills. My big-thinking ability made it possible for me to draft a job description for a position I would soon fill. Creating and believing I would fill this job that served all schools in sustaining positive school cultures was simply, well, miraculous. Well, I never! Me, drafting a handwritten proposal. New, not old ways. Authoring a playlist of mantras that would be at the ready in my backpack and practicing them while doing dishes would prep me for the sticky, tricky situations in my future daily walk. "I walk away from things that don't fit me. I release others. I shift, grow, and evolve." Mantras at the ready were not things of old. Roadblocks that impeded this idea of making a new, empowered self that were attempting to slither into my very soul with energy as foul as territorial serpents' morning breath were now things of old. Inviting my childlike self who collected heart rocks and made hair pieces by sticking flowers in her ponytail holder were now new.

Quantifying the infinitesimal shift upon the arrival and first months of Come Here You's presence in our home's energy is impossible. But, considering to consider is the first step in creating seismic shifts of the heart, of the mind, and of the soul. Could it be Come Here You was, dare I say, Jesus inviting me to consider?

Big honkin' miracles have names. There are the "Jesus Casting Out Unclean Spirits" and the "Great Haul of Fishes" miracles. One that did not receive much press was the "Raising of Jairus's Daughter from the Dead" miracle. Some people claim the "Jesus's Face in a Tortilla Chip" is a miracle. The "U.S. Airways Flight 1549 Emergency Landing on the Hudson River" miracle was pretty amazing in these them there modern times. We can't forget the "Immaculate Conception" miracle. Now, maybe, just maybe, we had the "Jesus in a Dog" miracle?

Regardless, this story is about dimes and a boy-turned-man, an otherworldly presence, and light entering into a space that was feeling a little like being in-between old ways and new ways. And snakes too.

Psalm 77:14 (NIV)
You are the God who performs miracles; you display your power among the peoples.

Step #17

Question Your Own Affairs

THE PUPPY'S NAMING CEREMONY WAS two days in length and chock-full of the Socratic method of questioning. In the process of considering the unimaginable impact her presence may have upon our lives, Teenager first needed to question his own affairs.

Before any naming ceremony could take place, Teenager's story of origin, values, beliefs, ancestral lineage, sense of purpose, evolutionary awareness, pride, life path, needs, hopes, choices, and his being-ness needed to be examined.

Privately, Teenager moved throughout two days in a state of reflection. There was no study session, no lists, no conversations—just Teenager walking with the responsibility of naming this otherworldly puppy upon his shoulders. Some ceremonies happen only inside of our being, similar to the transformation of the caterpillar in its cocoon. Or like choosing a name. Sometimes, the most epic moments of our lives occur with no pomp, no circumstance.

Teenager gathered his soul into a bucket and began to surface his life-altering stories into consciousness. He whispered thoughts and dreamt of what could become of this puppy. He thought in circles, walked in circles, remained open to metaphors and lessons from parables. He trusted his voice would surface in the quiet he provided.

Teenager was skilled at naming. I mean, Baby Snuggles? Come on now. Teenager needed a name for Come Here You that was universally known across many languages. After all, this pup was entering into Teenager's personal story that held within its pages a set of great-great grandparents that were deaf and another that spoke Polish. With Teenager, pup would want to celebrate the diversity of languages from his great-great-grandparent's visual language to Polish. Additionally, Teenager had grandparents that spoke Chicagoan and Budweiser Milwaukeean.

He needed a name that embraced his beliefs in a higher being, a presence that was love and energy, a higher power that sheds grace and offers second and third chances, a helping entity that gifts anew each day.

Honoring those that came before would support Teenager's choice in name and would open space for a pup to then continue to be who pup was supposed to be on this planet. This pup, Teenager knew, would become a part of his forever story, our collective ancestral lineage. Perhaps, just like Adam who named all the creatures, Teenager first had to recognize that this four-legged creature was God's creation.

After several sunrises and sunsets, Teenager took Come Here You within his wrestling-ripped arms that magically molded around each tiny paw, each curve of her supple belly, and her black-hearted imprinted face. He faced her outwardly so the world could embrace her enormous ears placed upon her serious countenance, and in a whisper barely audible announced, "Her name is Noel."

The name Noel was a result of Teenager diligently questioning his own affairs. Noel, a universally understood concept that means to be born. Noel, spoken in different languages yet with the same message of salvation: new.

This name Teenager had so thoughtfully chosen offered me sweet encouragement. Any time is a good time to question my own affairs even if I'm not engaged in a naming ceremony. What a beautiful manner in which to move from this season to the next. To bring the new front and center.

The new in Noel's name gave me new hope that an answer to my question about how to evict the snakes was around the corner, and a new possibility that a cure for my oregano-filled trauma was right over there. I remember looking at Noel's little being with her huge ears, one white, one black, and her oh-so-serious countenance and out of my mouth trickled an audible sigh and an, "I'm on the edge of transcendence."

In the space between the old and the new is where grace cometh. Noel. The grace has arrived? Noel's soul code is written in a language all her own and now adds to Teenager's list of lineage languages: dog language.

Noel. She is a stand-alone sentence. She is all the components that make for an eloquently woven declarative statement. Each letter within demands its own space. Implied are ellipses, question marks, and a message. Each letter, leaning upon the other, defines her wild spirit, her soft servanthood soul, and her cunning mind. She is N O E L. She embodies what it means to be an adjective, adverb, and prepositional phrase. If we look closely, right there, there's a dangling participle hanging off her right ear.

Noel. One name.

Genesis 2:20 (NIV)
So the man gave names to all the livestock, the birds in the sky, and all the wild animals.

Step #18

Know Who You Follow

DURING THE TWO-DAY NAMING NOEL retreat, there was a collective decision made to attach no strings to Noel's name. There were no suffixes given to Noel. No labels that would forever bind her to a particular role or state of being. No Miss, no Mrs., no Ms. No. There was no middle name and no last name. No Junior, Senior, or once-removed-step half-sister. No. There was only Noel. Noel in the beginning, Noel now, and Noel ever shall be. No, wait, that's a doxology about God. There was just Noel. Yes, just Noel. Until. Until her name became Noel the Dog of Many Names.

Only after Noel received her name did we realize that in the French language *joyeux Noel* means *merry Christmas*. And, heck, I know what Christmas means. Jesus came from Heaven in the form of a baby, and he lived the perfect (sin-free) life. (To be clear, it certainly was not a *perfect* life, I mean persecution, crowns with thorns...) He died a sinner's death and rose so we might be saved. So Noel means Christmas, which translates to Good News, redemption, and new life. Just like Jesus did when he entered a space, we began to witness a similar impact Noel had within spaces of the human experience. She, too, brought transformative new light and life.

When Jesus walked the Earth spreading the Good News, he would often share it with the locals he found along his path. I struggle, even today, to imagine Jesus just casually meeting me on a walk or getting water from the well where he would explain in simple terms what exactly His Good News was. Telling me that anyone can be forgiven and everyone can enter the kingdom by having faith in Jesus. I mean, that kind of chitty chat is bigger than just talking about the weather, now isn't it?

Often, these chitty chats would occur with folks after their raising the roof the night before or during their water gathering at the well. Jesus was a connector and went where the regulars were found. One time, he even ate bread with his BFFs and told them, "Take and eat; this is my body." Regardless of what Jesus did with others when they hung out together, those in his presence left with the Good News and with new life. They left transformed.

When Jesus walked this earth, there was no social media, no newspapers, no fancy. There was word of mouth only, and just like the game of telephone, the original messaging had the potential to get tainted as it went from ear to ear. I wonder if that's why Jesus's messaging was so simple. Less complicated messaging means less potential to mess with it too much. When Jesus joined a group of people at the local swim hole, I imagine he said something like, "Hey, I got some Good News."

Now who wouldn't grab a towel and come closer to hear more?

"The kingdom of God is here," he would've said, and just like a beloved pop star, he grabbed that microphone and dropped it right there on the sand.

I imagine goose-bumped swimmers leaning in toward one another and the questions swirling in their minds. *That's it? That's the Good News? It's not something out there for only the people who bought a ticket? It's here? Right here?* I bet those swimming-hole waders all looked at one another in their beach towels and a hush fell among them.

When Jesus left the swimmers on that sandy beach, perhaps, just maybe perhaps, He left them transformed or at least in a place to consider considering. I am confident after hearing the Good News and seeing the mic drop, someone broke that silent hush with a, "Well, I never."

Noel had many naming ceremonies in her life. These ceremonies often went unnoticed. She was renamed by some out of affection or a story or message she left. In the purest of moments, we might be caught calling her Welly, Well-Well, or Noelly. Sometimes, with super soupy, gooshy love, we called her Ah-Welly or Ah-Well.

Ah-Well. After dozens of times calling her Ah-Well, I suddenly realized, Ah-Well was just that. A well, where parched beings come to quench their thirst and gather with others. Just like the watering wells in ancient historic times, she too was the cornerstone of a community, albeit a tiny community, and she was indeed key to her community's sustainability.

As Teenager continued to mature, his appreciation for life-sustaining relationships grew. His thirst to be connected to others with whom he shared devotion built on authenticity, similar values, belief systems, and trust was real. I watched him make bonds outside of his tiny family that added to his bloodline. These relationships are, to this day, a part of the sustenance that quenches his thirst from the well.

I walked with Noel often in our neighborhood. One day, as we walked on the sidewalk, an old clackety-clunk car being driven by a teenager slowed, and from its window we heard, "HI NOELLL!"

This was a thing. This public acknowledgment happened often. Random cars with people I did not recognize would yell one of her many names out of their window. She would stop, look at the car, watch the car disappear, and continue her purpose-driven quick gate. No bragging. No surprise. No running into the road to chase the greeting. No startled disruption to what she was doing and where she was going. Just a soft moment of acknowledgement: *I heard them. They know me.*

Perhaps, if my gut tells me right, she knew them. Just as she knew any human who passed throughout her days. No one was a stranger, and her followers called her by name.

Before Noel was big, she was little. And before she made people gasp in awe at her prowess in fighting away predators, she was little. And yet, her messages were not. Not little. In an open, present, and willing stance, her young boy, who was now in midstream of his own transition to independence and testosterone-filled days, couldn't help but notice Noel's humble arrival as a baby and now a full-growner that had such remarkable impact in this space he called life.

John 14:7 (NIV)
If you really know me,
you will know my Father as well.

Step #19

Know Lost Is Found

NOEL WAS KNOWN TO VANISH when we ventured into the trees. She could not resist a wild run in the patch of forest that flourished just behind our house. She participated in games of chase with the local deer and speed competitions with the wind. When Noel ran, she was more airborne than not. Her ears pressed against the sides of her head to create an aerodynamic shape that allowed her to slip through the breeze. When Noel ran, she flew as a confident prairie hawk, navigating with ease the changes in wind currents. Noel ran with the wind through her first decade of development.

As Teenager developed his six-pack abs from smashing lacrosse balls into the varsity high school net, the two mirrored maturational growth. The only difference? Noel stood at two feet and Teenager at five feet, eight inches. There were many times in Noel's early years where her speed, core strength, endurance, and athletic ability stopped humans in their tracks. When Noel was running, there was nothing else. There was not hunger, wantonness, or wandering spirit. There was just running.

One snow-blizzard day, a crew of snow removal profes-
sionals showed up to tackle piles of the heavy, wet spring flakes
from the school parking lot Noel and I had started to explore
on foot. Me with my ice traction cleats attached to my boots,
Noel with her nothin' on. Noel advocated for herself in all
situations, including what four-legged athletes wear and what
they do not wear. She bound through drifts without so much
as earmuffs. While watching her swim within the drifts in the
snow-globe world, I suddenly had a flashback of one summer
day.

In Noel's early life, we bought her a new collar. We were
so excited. It was perfect for her athletic self and met all the
neighborhood regulations in the event we needed to put her
on a leash. The color, the width, and the tightly woven threads
made it baby-smooth to the touch. It was just big enough for
us to slip over her head without undoing the latch. Noel wore
collars like I wear a long necklace. She knew the rules.

The new collar was a shade of pink, and we agreed it was
a perfect color for her to wear out and about. Pink spoke with
quiet and humble authority. Gently, she was displaying her
gender to the world without being overly forthright. It hung
just above the collar bones, the sweet spot. After placing the
collar upon her, however, we noticed her posture sank a bit
and her eye-contact abruptly ended. The life seemed to have
been sucked from her being. She sauntered over to her hunting ottoman, hopped up, and peered out the window. The
cold shoulder had been cast.

Did we interrupt her hunting session? Was it the gender-
assigning pink that had caused her disdain? No. Dogs don't

know about gender identity conforming messaging. No. Couldn't be. She was a girl and that was that. Or was it?

I understand Jesus the King strolled around in street attire. He wore sandals and might have enjoyed longer hair. I imagine Jesus hoofing it up foothills to find the perfect place to project his voice. I imagine him standing in muddy earth preaching his message. I imagine him being blown about in desert wind as He claimed He is what they all had been waiting for. I imagine Jesus was a hard sell for some. He didn't look like a messenger in sandals with disheveled hair, and Noel didn't look like otherworldly wisdom either. Or, a girl, come to think about it.

The collar rules in our home were: 1) in public, we wear our name tag collar, and 2) inside, we go naked. She happily offered her head to us so we could slip her collar on before we ventured out into nature's playground. Even with her crunchy attitude about the pink collar, she understood the rules. Regardless of the color of her collar, when Noel was out and about, she was never ever, ever addressed as a dog of female gender.

"Oh, he's a funny good boy, isn't he?" folks would comment. "Look at him run!" and "Look at those big ears on him!" and "Hey, what kind of dog is he?"

A few months after the pink-collar cold shoulder episode, a new collar was presented to Noel. This collar was rich in purple tones with the same silky threads, same length, and same manufacturer. The purple collar was placed upon her, and she lifted her chest while her tail wagged. Dark purple was who she was.

A cartoon-sized snowflake landed on my eyeglasses as I stood in that pile of snow with Noel in nature's winter, my mind had wandered off to past collar memories. I shook a few flakes from my face and found myself standing on the snowy parking lot. Oh yes, the parking lot.

Apparently, the spring snow was so heavy one of the blades had broken on a crew member's plow truck. Five snow removal team members stood around the vehicle chatting about this dilemma as Noel and I navigated through the winter wonderland.

The crew observed naked, raw Noel bouncing and diving in snow drifts much deeper than she was tall. Like a pouncing deer, she would appear, dive in, and disappear. There was nothing easy about moving through snow one foot taller than oneself. Noel stood on tippy toes or rather, tippy paws. This work was not the work for a dog that wore hand-knitted sweaters and sported painted nails.

The bundled crew tick-tocked their heads in unison as they observed her flying over piles of snow. If I listened closely, I could almost hear the wind shiver from her rapid passing.

Suddenly, a coyote appeared out of the caves of the frozen trees and shrub oak that covered a steep hill outlining the parking lot's north end. Behind the wall of snow-covered dense shrub was the forest that housed squirrel, buck, coyotes, bear, and acres of open space. Some seventy-five feet from where we stood, I saw a coyote peering fierce intent upon me, the snowplow crew, and Noel. My heart accelerated and cortisol raced through my veins. Fight? Flight? Noel's white hair camouflaged her in the Colorado neon-white snow. In a flash, Welly darted up a steep foothill in pursuit of the coyote while keeping her head down to hide her black-hearted face. From our bystander perspective, she seemed to have disappeared in her pursuit.

Now, I knew coyotes hunt in packs, and when they find an animal that is vulnerable, one coyote may entice it to move closer to the pack where the others prepare to circle the prey. When Noel's black-hearted face disappeared, I feared. At that moment, a crew man yelled to me, "Hey, was that a dog? After a coyote! Well, I never."

Me either, Snow Man. Me either.

I knew when those men got back to their lunchroom at work they told the story of a dog who bounded through snow drifts, lightening quick, to chase a predator away. I wonder if they were impacted having witnessed her fire, her passion, her light, her wisdom, her joy exploded upon her space and all those in it. Over their lunch break sandwiches, I think maybe the snow men group was transformed a bit. I know all it takes for me to grow and evolve just a tiny bit is seeing something that I believe is a bit too miraculous. I mean after all, "I never."

Before I could gather my breath to call her name, she reappeared. Tumbling down the hill she came, stump-tail wagging as she lowered her head. Breathing fast enough to make her little muscled body bounce with each inhale, with head lowered and tongue moving to the cadence of her rapidly beating heart, she sauntered up to the crew, huddled in their circle around the broken truck, and like a long-lost friend, plopped herself down on the ice, ears in complete submission. She panted and smiled through that serious countenance in a way only Noel could do. She whispered, "I am here."

I'll never really know what happened in that snowy forest the day she ran with the coyote. I will never know if she scolded it, simply watched the cunning coyote run into the distance, or took his name and put him on her list. What I do know is she was protecting the crew who was wildly unaware of her skill and drive. The crew had never given her a treat, didn't know her name, and had never had her over for dinner. Yet there she was, mustering up the prowess within to do what she was called to do in that very moment: to serve, protect, and be her badass self.

When Noel ran, she ran like the wind, chasing away danger and forever attempting to beat her own pace. When she ran, her soul was home. When she turned the tables on that coyote, she was in chase of something bigger than what is here. When Noel ran after things in caves and dark spaces with wild abandon, it often appeared she may lose her way, as if she may not know the path. Yet, miraculously, she always, always returned. I guess, when we know where our own soul's home is, we are never lost. We are found, we are home. While observing Noel chase after a predator, I believed she may have gotten lost in her pursuit. After the coyote incident, and time to chew on the event, I began to welcome an idea that later would comfort me through this life transition and more to come. When I am feeling lost as I shift from being this person to that person, I need to stay steadfast in chasing the predators away. Predators such as an apathetic approach to my crafting and designing a new way to live and fear of failure when trying new behaviors. Apathy and fear—oh, most definitely predators. I must chase those stinkin' coyotes right up that hill, into the forest with head held high and tongue out to absorb all the air I possibly can. For, when I am in the forest, I am actually found. Just like Welly. Yes, just like Welly.

But this story is not about snowplow crews and coyotes. This story is about dimes and a boy-turned-man, an other-worldly presence, light entering into a space that was feeling a little gloomy-ish, and snakes too.

Luke 15:24 (NLT)
He was lost, but now he is found.

Step #20

Heed That Whisper Within

WHEN JESUS WAS A CHILD, He attended a multiple-day festival with his family. As the festival was ending, Jesus quietly strayed from his parents. His parents were sure he was under the care of others in the group who were as thick as family. When Jesus was still missing on the last night of the festival, His parents began to frantically (okay, my word, sure, but frantic is how it feels when kids go missing, yes?) search. Later they found Him in the local Temple sitting among religious teachers and elders.

All of the teachers were amazed at Jesus's understanding of the lessons and were astounded by his answers. When Jesus's parents approached Him, they were upset, to put it mildly, and most likely visibly shaken. Jesus looked at them with surprise at their displayed emotion. "How is it you sought me? Did you not know that I must be in my Father's house?"

Despite the celebratory vibe, the dancing, the sharing of good food, and the rich conversation happening at the festival, Jesus was called deep within His heart to leave the party. He went to where he felt most authentically himself. He was drawn by the very spirit within Him to go forth. There was a purpose and a place where His teachings could sit among others. His stepping away from the festivities was not in disregard. He was drawn as the rising tide is to sand. The magnetic draw was so strong, and it was simply Him heeding His purpose and mission. When His parents were reunited with him, I am certain, the Temple leaders could say very little beyond the whisper of His name and maybe a gentle, "Yes, Mary, He is here. Jesus is here. His name is Jesus. Jesus, Almighty Teacher."

I wonder if Mary grabbed His tiny arm after His Temple-shenanigan moment and squeezed it with pursed lips like Libby did to me and my sister. It's very possible. If you have lost a child or a beloved animal, you can relate to the trauma that instant panic causes within any loving parent's heart—the sweaty palms, the escape of all breath, and the unbridled fear. As Mary and Joseph escorted (maybe gently dragged) Jesus back to the festival, perhaps they were referring to him as Mud.

Like Noel, or rather like Jesus, Noel came to have many names. Jesus was also known in the land as Only Begotten Son, Savior, Counselor, King of Kings, Alpha and Omega, Advocate, Rock, The Way, The Truth and The Life, The Word, Friend, Son of God, Yahweh, and more. More and more and more names.

Sometimes, one name, like Jesus, is plenty and speaks volumes. One name with no suffixes, no title, no more. Plato. Aretha. Prince. Steinbeck. Cher. Marge. Shakespeare. Libby. Noel. Sometimes, the one-named, as in Jesus's case, was never just that one name. It had to be this one name and then that one name because one name did not encompass all they were to everyone who went seeking.

Noel was Noel. Until she was Welly, as you know. And Well-Well and Leon (which is a whole other story about how her human grandfather's name was Leon, which happens to be Noel backwards, which Teenager did not realize until she was already so named!). Grandfather Leon is the traveler man who Teenager was named after. Did Teenager or anyone else realize any of this in her naming ceremony? No. It's a God thing. That is how we categorize that cosmic connection. Mononyms are so simple; their power is miraculous.

As Jesus walked this earth, His impact upon us and among us was and still is defined through his many names. Those that got to witness his human-form presence, His hyper-focused way of carrying out His messaging of the Good News, and His sermons, teachings, and healings were radically transformed, and many referred to Jesus as the Messiah. Oh my goodness, there's another name. The one with many names.

I too have had that panicked response that Mary and Joseph potentially had several times when I turned my back for a moment and Noel was gone during one of our wild forest walks. In hindsight, I suppose all she was doing was heeding a calling from the wind within in her spirit. And, in heeding the call, she was at home. She was not lost. Home is within. The way is the path and the way is home.

After Well-Welly's run with the coyote and my recollection of the Temple story, I gained refreshed perspective. How can anyone get angry at a boy who wants to hang out with leaders in the Temple with intent to humbly teach those elders a thing or two about love at the age of about nine or ten? How can anyone get upset at a dog for running up a snowy slope after a coyote? How can any person feel sidelined when their son grows up and has two wings and one foot out of the nest?

Heeding the call can fend off predators. Heeding the voice of Spirit within can help me morph and evolve after each stage has ended in my life. Heeding the whisper within prepares me for the place I will call *home* on my future walking path.

Luke 2:49 (NIV)
Why were you searching for me? Did you not know I had to be in my Father's house?

Step #21

Make Room – Rid Your Space

As the days turned to weeks and weeks morphed into months and years, I watched Welly's hair become course and the dark black heart on her face closed its bottom point. I often reflected upon my own change that occurred day after day, month to month and later, year to year. The deeper I observed Ah-Well-Well's confident transition that led her to morph into her evolved self, I witnessed more and more how everything she did and everything she exceled in was coming from a deeper pull from within. She did not fall to societal messaging and did not crawl into boxes that stifled her true identity. Unlike Noel, I had a history of walking a fine tight rope of things I should not do and things I should do. There is a fine piece of rope separating the choosing of a life verses the allowing of life to choose me.

I sat criss-cross applesauce on my yoga mat attempting to create a free and clear space. A space where memories and past choices I made were on hiatus. I thought if I could pull just some of the past into this moment, perhaps I could discern when I chose my life choices and when I simply let life choose me. If I separate the intention from all the other noise, I might be able to summon my way-maker wisdom. The longer I sat, the cramps became almost unbearable. I did not create a Zen-like space. The only deep pull I felt was in my hamstrings and hip joints.

One criss-cross applesauce yoga mat memory did surface and brought visions of beautiful wooden pews, stained glass, and heavy church doors. My sister and I were born in front of the time clock, ready to punch in. As a daughter of a highly successful clergy, I was born to work, to flit about as any good hostess does at any party. I was born to illuminate. Illuminate the cheese casserole in God's light as I gave Mrs. Methodist a plop of funeral mac and cheese at the memorial service. Illuminate the rows and rows of pews after Sunday's service by straightening all the hymnals, nose tissues, Bibles, and handwritten leftover love notes about what Sunday night football will look like after service with beer, foot rubs, and ecstasy. As a preteen, I imagined ecstasy was most likely ice cream during halftime. Sliding across each pew was the ecstasy while cleaning and organizing the church pews. That I knew. Oh, and I knew I was not spiritually called or pulled to illuminate the church parking lot on Saturdays by sweeping the rice away after guests threw it at the trillions of newlyweds as they ran to their cars decorated with soup cans. I reported to work because. Because. No choice.

In high school, I began to explore the yin and yang energy between what was *right* and what my strong desire was. Looking back, I suppose some of my desires were not *right* either, but it was a period of time where I craved the experience of the power of pull from a little voice within. I was practicing adhering to a calling. Me, a skilled member of the pom-pom team (right) who attended a kegger party before our performance (a strong pull, um, probably a no). Typically, I drove the 1977 two-door Honda Civic within speed limits (right) but carried my four best girlfriends in the hatchback (no, no, no).

In college, I excelled academically and socially and, I know you know, I spent many an evening at the railroad track parties. In hindsight, I can see that as I progressed through my college years, the voice within became more prominent. I associated this voice with the real me.

With closed eyes, I could see Mr. Kent's balding head. I remembered the day Mr. Kent threw the van keys to me in my sophomore year of college. He led our traveling theater group, and one day, due to illness, he could not drive. He entrusted me to get our troupe to the next gig. Apparently, Mr. Kent saw a spark of maturity seeping out of my being. He had to have known he was taking a risk, and he had to have known that trusting me would only help me to blossom further. When he tossed the keys to me I whispered a new mantra, "I'm creative, brave, and rock-star cool," while my eyes misted over. Somehow, in the middle of my crazy college life, I began to chase some of my predators away. Space was opened for growth. Seen by a professor who was sick and who asked me, of all people, to drive the van. In doing more right, right for me and my purpose, I was able to truly illuminate.

My first professional job after college graduation was teaching nineteen-year-old seniors in high school. I was twenty-two years old. Twenty-two. These were resilient, inner-city kids and most had children they were raising at home. In their enormously huge high school was a subculture of gangs. Gangs. Maybe more concerning than aneurysms and snakes? The school was in lockdown all day, and when the morning bell rang, the doors were gated and locked. Chaos. Each morning as I combed my I'm-just-three-years-older-than-you-guys teacher hair, I spoke to my predators. *Listen here, fear and doubt, you don't scare me. Look at me! I'm creative, brave, and rock-star cool.* Without curriculum or mentoring, I was given freedom to offer the students what I thought was important. I offered my students life. I read them poems and invited them to dictate their words to me. We colored and spoke. Real conversations. Real fellowship. We spoke of heart rhythms and generated written, spelled correctly, lists of all the stupid things in our lives. We shared snacks, and I made enough mac and cheese one day that everyone got a plop. We opened space to think, to rap, to dance, and write.

Near the end of my first year of teaching, the principal, who I hadn't talked to all year, called me to his office. We sat together at a tiny desk, I remember. A piece of paper was on the table. "I don't know what you're doing down there, but I hear they're showing up." He offered me my teaching contract renewal. I spun the paper around so it was facing him again and slid it back to him across the pinewood surface unsigned.

"Oh, thank you," I nervously giggled. "But I can't ever come back here again." That decision was only right in one way. It may not have been pretty, but my voice spoke wisdom, and I trusted my voice. I heeded the calling from within to continue exploring the next season of my life. I certainly had evolved in just one school year. Now that, that was right. Creating a space to walk away and grow again. Right.

Throughout my son's last year in public school, I was well aware that Noel had become my companion and somewhat of a second child. I had fond memories of her as a babe, just as I did of my human son. As a baby, Noelly did not announce the first time she planned to attack the ant on the carpet by placing it ever so gently in her lips. Yes, lips. She did not refer to her daily agenda, she did not ask permission, she simply just did. With ant in mouth, she shook her head back and forth with a force unknown to the human neck. Violently, she shook that innocent ant to the right then to the left, and when something within her paused for a breath, she knew. She knew. It was done. The tiny ant was released from her lips, fell upon the floor lifeless, soul ascended, a carcass. Noel had simply done what she was called to do. She. Broke. Its. Neck.

And there it was.

Evidence of her higher calling? It happened so suddenly and effortlessly. It was as if I could hear the pounding within her heart as the cells within her very body united with her cognitive and neurological messaging system. Without training or mentoring or studying, she grabbed that intruder, took her tiny teeth around its neck and, well, you know.

You can imagine the horror. With the teeny-tiny ant legs strewn across my carpet, her gentle eyes met mine. What in good gracious earth just happened? In a dog-whisper nano-second, I felt her words fall upon the moment, "It's okay. We are safe now." As time passed and she grew, in front of my very eyes, Noel began to hone her masterful break-its-neck skill.

How would I put love around such an incident, I pondered. If only I had known her erratic, concerning, gross, shocking, bewildering, purpose-driven behavior was coming from a place so deep within her soul. Before her body, before her entrance into this world, and before we opened the knock at the door, this calling had been created within her.

What Noel was doing was a result only, a result of her practicing the use of the map that lay imprinted within her very DNA. In all of my days, I suppose, I too was practicing for the next—the next curve, the next valley, the next hill. This simple yet profound enlightenment stirred a bit of regret. Regret that perhaps I had spent a day too long wandering or feeling resentment or wishing for something that was not mine to be had. I vowed, now was the best time to begin accessing the practice I had done previously in the life seasons of my teens, twenties, and thirties. To once again craft a purpose-driven next life-trail to walk upon. I promised more illumination that would come from moments that allowed my skill to surface. More time to play with the energy of yin and yang—the ultimate metaphor for life-force balance. More peace, less predators. More effort in creating space to walk away and start again. Purpose driven, dang it.

I continued to watch Noel develop her break-its-neck skills as she gradually increased her size of predator. She moved from ants to stuffed animals to kitchen spatulas and ropes. Each time, her lips and paws worked together at the speed of light to locate the neck. As she worked, I found myself shaking my head with her to ward off those past feelings of regret. Hey you, Regret. Yes, you. Yes, you who I name Regret. Come here and I'll break your neck!

The whispering winds within our heads and hearts that speak direction to us are not violent nor harmful to souls. These directions are only reflections of our soul's code. This inner voice to act at times, or simply to just be inside of the ordinary or mundane that a simple beautiful day can offer, is the gentle, magnetic force that directs, points the way, and shows the path. This inner voice is my friend, my way maker, and in heeding and allowing permission to play with this friend, I will walk as a child in the light again. Look at me, Mr. Kent. Permission to play again. Absolutely radical. Protection, love, support, growth, connectedness, influence, and the betterment of the globe are all just results of the callings within.

Sometimes, this answering of our soul's code can look like breaking its neck to rid a space of dark intruders, emptiness, wandering spirits, or chaos that can encroach in the in-between.

Ephesians 5:8 (NIV)
For you were once darkness, but now you
are light...walk as children of light.

Step #22

Prepare for Radical Transformation

MONTHS WERE ZOOMING BY AT the speed of light. Boy grew, work demands continued to suck sixty hours a week from my treadmill-running self. When I was surface-living, it seemed collars and snakes and Saturday morning sports games started to blur together. Snakes continued to slither and leave me with nightmares many evenings. Yet, in the midst of my autopilot and treadmill ways, my slowly evolving self was abandoning dishtowel after dishtowel shroud.

I realized, in the quiet and privacy of the bathroom, I was beginning to walk in new light with new consideration. My recently developed behaviors were not yet self-evident, but my thinking was shifting, and I began to actually hear some of my own thoughts. Tree spirit whisperings spoke: *Your life is made of seasons.*

Through my observations of Noel's many thoughtful approaches to her own life, I had indeed begun to shift my perspective for my own life. I welcomed a bit more responsibility in stepping off of the autopilot treadmill, and I began to daydream of diving into snowbanks and seeking the calling within that would then shape this next season of life. I began to consider taking the stench and translucent skin from the basement dwellers by the neck and breaking, well, you know.

The first encounter between Noel and our resident snakes was traumatizing.

The first snake that appeared in flesh and blood inside of the home where we slept, ate, showered, studied, cleaned, and lived was found on the tile floor of Teenager's bathroom. As I flipped the restroom light on in an attempt to awaken said teenager for the fifth time as he and Noel slept under the covers, I screamed. I screamed to the angels responsible for helping in the we-are-all-going-to-die moments, and I cursed every scaly, red beady-eye, and tongue-waggle approaching too close to my ankle with words a potty-mouth is even ashamed of. I jumped and stomped and lost my place as if a tsunami had suddenly risen from the bowels of my being.

With quivering lip and heart racing, I stared at the writhing serpent on the tile floor and felt a rumble rise within my heart, allowed it to pass through my throat, and into my mouth.

"NOOOELLLL!"

And there she appeared. She jumped out of Teenager's comforter, fumbled her way to the bathroom in her still developing body, pursed her lips just so, and within a blink of an eye the deed was done. After the last breath of the snake had escaped, she sat upon the tile, yawned a tiny puppy yawn, looked into my eyes, and mental telepathized me, *"It's okay now. We can all go back to bed."*

Then, in a nanosecond, I heard these words travel from her mind to mine, "*No need to worry, I'm safe, we are all safe. I'm in my Father's house. I'm home.*"

I watched Noel scoochy by my traumatized, standing-on-cold-bathroom-tile self. I was paralyzed and could not bend to pick her up to wash her baby belly off after the ruthless act she had committed. All I could do is listen to the wind within my soul. *When I do what I'm supposed to do, I'm in my Father's house. If what I am doing appears to be somewhat scary and a bit off-putting, no matter. Heeding the purpose for my life-calling may require courage and sweat equity. It may offend others on the outside or seem out of juxtaposition with how the world works, but if I am doing what I feel I should be doing, I'm in my Father's house.*

Looking at the bloody carcass of the snake on the tile floor; I knew Noel's presence had been presented to us as a gift. Her presence in our home was to shake the darkness into light and support a smooth transition from life with snakes to life after snakes. Her presence in our home was, dare I say, a tiny miracle?

She was here to model a new way to move beyond one period of life to the next. She also was sent to teach the boy and his family and friends, his community, lacrosse coach, tennis buddies, and the cul-de-sac a thing or two about this daily walk we are all on. She was here to break its neck and teach me how to remove bloody snake remains from a tile floor, white tiled walls, dog ribs, and cheeks. After this first snake encounter, I prepared myself for radical inward revolution.

Somehow, I was deeply moved by her grotesque behavior with that unfortunate shower-squatting snake. I was shaken, disturbed, disgusted, and inspired. I also wanted to yell messages of empowerment and self-advocacy from the bottom of my being into the space I called Teenager's bathroom.

She had come to create a sanctuary of sorts, right here in the restroom. She had come to infiltrate every space of my brick-and-mortar home, but most importantly, my home within. Watching her break that snake's neck was horrifying, and the behavior was perhaps inappropriate. It was a violent act, but it came from a space of protection.

Noel rid our residence and property of each and every one of the hundreds of slithering snakes that lived in our home. It sure was not pretty finding snake carcasses all over the yard day after day. There were many baths and chats as we scrubbed pieces of the bloody battle from her fur daily. It's not a scene we associate with her profound love, her gentle spirit, and her will to live the best life ever. But, after all, Welly had her pack to protect and love. She arrived when the snake stench in our house was unavoidable. In due time, she alone conquered.

Perfect timing, right?

Much happens in quiet spaces like bathrooms. Life shifts behind the scenes and teeny tiny events occur in bits and fragments. Like puzzle pieces, we can study our old ways, explore feelings, and use some of the old ways to mold our new.

Upon her arrival, word spread quickly in the snake community. I am certain, behind the scenes of the HOA meeting, word was spreading in the snake community. There was some four-legged creature that was telling a new story that included some serpent-free piece of good news. It's said that one of the snakes later published a piece in the Snake Press that claimed one long ago day, a savior of sorts had arrived in Teenager's bathroom in the form of a d-o-g.

When Jesus came to walk with us among the trees and hills and upon our sidewalks made of gravel, He was so stunningly different than what we all expected. We kept hearing that some savior was coming. Now, I don't know how many ears that message of a new messiah went through, but by the time it fell upon the last few ears, this savior was supposed to actually save us, so the story went. I'm not sure how that message was whispered from neighbor to neighbor, but the one piece of communication that stayed the same was that He was coming. He was coming to hang out with us. To eat with us, sleep in our barns with us, chat with us, laugh with us. SO, you can imagine, when he showed up as a baby and then an apprentice carpenter and farmer from a tiny town, there was a lot of head scratchin' goin' on.

What he preached was so radical from what we had been hearing. We were accustomed to following rules and sacrificing animals and not eating meat on certain days, and, oh my, lions and tigers and bears. Oh my! But when Jesus came, he called for a radical inward (yes, inward) transformation in each one of us. His ask was that simple: invite Him into our hearts. Seems so easy-peasy, really.

This baby in a manger who looked nothing like a powerful friend and savior invited us to simply admit this world is bigger than us. This baby just wanted me to admit that I need help, I make mistakes, and I am not able to live by free will alone. This baby who certainly could be nothing more than a b-a-b-y invited relationship. He wasn't asking us to cling to old knick-knacks or coupons, or dimes. He was gifting us with the promise of never leaving us, peace, rest, and eternal life. Now that, my friend, is radical, man.

And a d-o-g teaching me about how to create spaces of sanctuary? Sanctuary. A sacred gap, like the opening when the body is in between its exhale and inhale. A sacred instant between the birth of the babe and it's first audible breath. It's in this quiet sanctuary time, after we break a neck, sit upon the tile floor, and sigh that silence arrives. No where to go. No where to be. Just here. For a minute. A d-o-g, encouraging me to know my heart again so I can engage in radical transformation. I scarce can take her presence.

I paused and scratched my head. Well, I never.

Psalm 139:23–24 (NIV)
Search me, God, and know my heart; test me and know my anxious thoughts. See if there is any offensive way in me, and lead me in the way everlasting.

Step #23

Recognize the Constant in Change

JUST AS JESUS MATURED RIGHT in front of his awe-struck parents, Welly did too, alongside her boy. Teenager entered his final year of summer vacation after high school graduation. Teenager's transitional wandering was quelled as the two of them worked through life's most difficult situations.

The term *difficult* is defined differently each life season. Difficult morphs as we mature and as we take on increasingly growing challenges. What I thought difficult in my thirties is no longer. In midlife, difficult was losing a friend way too early and grieving the loss of my parents in just barely my forties. Difficult was navigating my way through countless bosses that were increasingly younger and less professionally seasoned as I due to their limited time on the Earth. Difficult for a teen was forming bonds with friends that would eventually split due to future plans and dreams. Difficult to Teenager was spreading those wings and navigating his way through peer dynamics and pressure to perform on the field. Noel and Teenager shared the difficulty of having solid ground and then being pulled away from their mamma—nature's order.

They shared a bed and a love of nature. The boys on the lacrosse and tennis teams saw the two together frequently. The Red Rocks, Colorado, concert brotherhood knew the two traveled together as much as possible. They were indeed brothers, or rather, brother and sister, or gosh, does it matter? They were connected. They shared secrets and bliss while floating on rivers and camping under the stars. They were one. On cool summer evenings, the two would discuss Teenager's impending departure to college that would take him miles and mountain passes away. As Teenager's independence expanded, spending a full day with her very busy boy became more and more of a treat and yet, when the two were not together, their spirits were one.

Ah-Well's unadulterated love for him expanded throughout the last days of summer vacation and in the in-between transition to college days. He was going from teen to independent student where the stakes were never higher. With bated breath, I counted each day and felt the chaos begin to stir within my soul again. My identity was once again required to shift, my role of mom entering new territory again.

Time passed rapidly, and I walked in a fog while clinging to mists of memories that provided calm and structure. I worked long days, attended exercise class, and experienced sleepless nights filled with to-do lists and emails. All served as a great diversion to the sanctuary I did not so much want to find myself in.

The day came. The boxes of tie-dyed T-shirts, Grateful Dead-stickered water bottles, Chacos, and favorite pillows were stuffed into Teenager's car that would take him peaks, hairpin turns, and highway markers away to start his next life adventure. When Teenager left to explore the world of academia, I was left with no boy, and yet, the two, Noel and Teenager, remained so connected there were days I felt as if talking with Noel was like talking to Son's spirit. They were one in the same, and when I asked Welly what she thought her boy was doing today out in that big ol' world, she would stop at the sound of his name. Then, she would run to retrieve her flattened toy snake and shake it vigorously. "*There, I broke its neck.*"

Yes, sometimes we have to take feelings too big for words and break their necks, Noel, yes, yes, I get it.

Noel, too, had entered a new moon phase. The first gray hair appeared in the middle of her heart face. Her days were a bit quieter, and she changed sleeping arrangements after Boy entered college. The house was absent of testosterone teens. Her coping-skills wisdom began to display itself in miraculous new ways. She began to schedule her days. Scheduled was the water she needed and the nutrition her body craved. She exercised furiously each day, and if the daily strenuous runs, play sessions, and hunting was not adequate, she sufficed by adding zoomies. She displayed keen recognition when I was ill. Out of complete juxtaposition of who she was on the daily, she was able to recognize slight changes in my physical and emotional health. If a three-day sleep with my bronchitis self was required, she hopped on my bed and left her observational post for only her basic needs.

Noel's daily regimented agenda became a new way for her to help herself. She was intentionally weaning herself from routines of old as she reinvented herself. She worked diligently to fill the gap the absence of her boy left within her soul and within her home. She found things that still filled her world in ways that felt like deep connection and love.

I was inspired by Noel. I spent time each week finishing that job proposal I was going to pitch. I put time in my calendar to explore the outdoors each day so I could find the sacred messaging that comes from the metaphors in nature. I scheduled meditation, exercise, vision-board making, and sit-time where I lingered in the company of myself for five minutes a day. I got an exercise accountability partner and we still, even today, text one another to share the body-movement we did that day. I created Tiny Tuesday where I began reading or listening to a tiny new thought. How wild it was to let go for a teeny minute to hear a Buddhist teaching or to read Mary Oliver's words dance on the page her poetry graced. I designated a symbolic burial site in the middle of a patch of trees near my home to drop things I needed to release.

As a parent, we guide, lead, and teach our children so that eventually we can gently push them out of the nest. This weaning takes great prowess, and if parents do it right, they recognize the somewhat annoying teen years are all part of the natural cycle of parenthood. Eventually, the child weans themselves enough, so they alone can find their own way and care for themselves. In nature's order, there comes a time for them to stretch their lives, to move beyond the place of receiving good advice from others who had a hand in setting their foundation values and moral compass to crafting their own journey by following their own inspired wisdom. Follow their own God-given calling in the shell of their authentic self. None of this is pretty or easy, but brave parents and guardians know this is the natural order of things.

To be the Marge she became and to be the tire changer dude that he became, there had to have been several soft, gentle moments of weaning where they found their amazing selves. I mean, gosh. Marge sure had a lot of wisdom to share with other folks. Wisdom that came as a result of some struggles and soul-wandering, challenges and triumphs. Wisdom that came from bad jobs and sanctuary time. When she punches the time clock now, as a wise and seasoned Marge, she changes lives. Marge must have considered considering many things related to the evolution of herself. She crafted her own life with the help of the spirit within, found sanctuary space to breathe in potential, surrendered some of her old ways, purged the old shrouds of limited thinking she put upon herself, and accepted the responsibility to relocate her authentic self within her changed body. She saw light in the path that was set before her, and she put that apron on and knew she had the wisdom to influence. Marge walked many paths as she left one life-phase to another. Holy cow, Marge. You did this thing.

As my son grew, it was only natural for him to expand beyond home base so he could practice walking on the trail that was uniquely and only his. As Teenager reached and expanded, he also transformed. And all the while I was at home base transforming too. I was designing, sitting criss-cross applesauce on my mat and was replacing oh so many meeting agendas with sacred walk agendas. Consciously, I avoided the work lounge and purged many old expectations I had of other humans to lessen my disappointment and accept them more fully for who they were. None of these new ways were easy. It took intention and practice and a little me-first-time mentality. Me and Welly first. And Welly? She had already seamlessly transcended from sister of her boy to sister with far away boy.

Teenager's life led him into less-traveled circles. Circles in all directions. He began within the world of academia and the exploration of his place in it at college. He then found bliss in travel with a backpack, a few bucks, and a thumb. He worked outdoor education, slept in cars, and called a campground his home. He painted visions under stars.

Jesus was fully aware that a part of His walk was weaning us from having his presence in flesh and blood on Earth. While He walked with us in physical form, He spent gobs of energy explaining far out concepts. He shared suppers with those that needed healing and a path. He modeled compassion and taught us how to change the oil in our cars. I mean, fish. He taught us how to fish. He taught and taught and gave and gave and loved and loved and healed and promised us all a really great future. I mean, really great.

When Jesus began to prepare us for His evolution in presence, one of His strategic actions was to anoint some to continue to lead the effort of spreading His teachings. When I look back on my own Noel story, I see that the relationship between Teenager and dog was similar to Jesus's efforts to prepare us earth-walkers for His transformation. It was necessary that we understood that Jesus's actual human presence would cease to exist in mortal form, but the love and connection never would. The transcendence after the stage of having Jesus on Earth with us to then being humans that had their Messiah present in a different form had to happen. It was the natural order of things.

Before Jesus left us earth-walkers, he had already planted the Good News. When he left Earth, He had transformed to a new way of being in this world. We were transformed too. He promised, despite his new form, we would not walk alone.

My evolutionary thinking brought an awareness that life shifts, jobs change, relationships flow, and paths evolve. Nothing is stagnant, it ebbs and flows and transforms. However, love is still love. Welly knew. Love is always love even if he no longer wore dread locks or lived in the same house. Love is still love even in what can feel like far away.

Ecclesiastes 3 (NLT)
For everything there is an appointed time,
a time for every matter under heaven.

Chant Words of Wisdom

WELLY KNEW SELF-CARE. I DON'T know where she learned all that stuff. Not once did I see her reading a book. Alright, well once. Noel and I went to visit her boy who was dabbling into his new-found college life. Bearded Teenager had developed in ways we don't ever expect. He wore broader shoulders and his hands were more hands. While at college, he marveled at his new social life, mountains, and nature's expansive invitation. Welly loved a good road trip, and as we got closer to his college town, she could smell the subtle differences in climate and trees.

Academic inspiration was second on Noel's boy's list, and first priority was his insatiable appetite for human connection in the midst of nature. When we arrived on campus, Noel stuck her head out the window to observe the soon-to-be young adults in the streets dancing their way to here and there. Grateful Dead tattoos were proudly displayed, bohemian dresses blew gently in the breeze, and carabiner clips hung from backpacks. Noel's bit of a tail wiggled back and forth. She knew he was here. These were his people and her pack.

Noel and I checked into our, um, motel. Our temporary housing was in the heart of campus and had housed many snowboarders and three-day-festival attendees. Noel couldn't care less if there were suspect soap bars in the bathroom and stained brown carpet under the queen bed-ish. She inspected for snakes. None.

As soon as Teenager arrived at our front door, she sensed him on the other side. While jumping and wiggling at his appearance, she grabbed her toy and showed her displaced, overwhelming emotions. In her secret way she began to speak to him. She shared stories of our road trip and told about the deer outside her back window at home. She shared with him that she had brought her ball so they could play in the park. The two hugged and giggled, and it was as if not a day had passed. Welly had forgiven him for leaving and knew this was simply a part of his journey. Not a stitch was dropped as they fell into their roles with one another.

Her boy had been carrying a book upon his entering our hippie-wannabe den. By the looks of the book cover, it was a story about the Earth. A book to invite deep reflection while offering an opportunity for the reader to consider their place in this world. My son shared that he had been very busy and had not yet done the assigned reading. Noel sat upon his outstretched legs, listening to his plight. There was, after all, very much to do in college. There was river floating and mountain biking. Lacrosse, concerts, tent camping, and, oh yes, class assignments. This was all a part of his weaning journey, and I found I was practicing a new parenting role by giving permission to myself to surrender any displaced worry I may have about his academics. His story, not mine, I told myself.

I shook my head from the right to the left. This transitional stage of trying to learn how to be a mom of a soon-to-be young adult was one of the shifts I had intentionally vowed to begin making. I grabbed my thought inside of my lips and broke its neck.

Ah-Well listened to his plight as a good therapist did. They played ball and enjoyed snacks together. Soon after, Teenager left for the night. Noel hopped up onto the bed, saw his novel lying upon the paper-thin bed cover, and purposefully placed her head upon the book. She closed her eyes and began, what I believe, was a process of osmosis. It was as if she was saying, "His struggle is mine. His triumph is mine." Never apart. One.

I remember taking a picture of Noel with her head upon the Earth book and thinking, *Gosh, evolution and weaning and transcendence are harder than college, dang it.* For me. And perhaps a little for Well-Well.

Okay, so besides that hotel Earth book, I did not see Noel once reading a book or listening to a podcast about ways to improve her life or her ability to think about the Earth on a universal level. She did not need teachings or college classes to learn how to manifest joy and magical moments of self-care even while transitioning confidently from this stage of life to that stage. She *was* self-care. The elements that made up her whole dog-hood—mind, body and soul—were never separate. Somehow, she knew. Like a meditation guru or shaman or a wholistic healer, Noel knew. Mind, body, and spirit are symbiotic in relation. One falls? The other picks up. One triumphs? The other two celebrate. Just as the spirit speaks with the mind, and the mind knows how to guide the body, her complete self always led the way for her.

Each time Noel and I said goodbye to the teenager after our visit, I drove with tears, and Noel cuddled in her passenger seat wrapped in a blanket. Sometimes, I could hear her breathing. I would place my hand upon her back as her breath came in and slipped out. After much practice, we surrendered and simply agreed to accept our quiet resolve on the road trip home. We slowly began to embrace this difficult gap period now in our present lives.

I recall marveling at Welly's daily intentional choices to nurture herself and to connect when connection was far. Finding myself tapping into her as a role model became a real thing for me. Noel's process was always purposeful and always filled with faith that what she desired would come. Whether she was on a road trip to see her boy or at home waiting for the next time she would see her boy, she accepted her current state and took full responsibility to walk in the knowingness that she was never alone.

Moving, growing older, death and births, marriages, divorces profoundly alter our relationships, hence, our worlds. When our children find a life partner we may discover our place in line changes. This opens up space for exploring how to spend time alone. When a friend dies, the many now-missing shared rituals, holidays, traditions, and hours on the phone leave a Grand Canyon gap. This opens up space to learn how to fill the void.

Noel's way of progressing through transition got me thinking about how I was progressing. And boy howdy, did I spend time thinking about the shifts that should occur in my parenting style. As parents, we must find ourselves in a place one day where we trust to release the reins. We trust our adult child to carve their own path and believe they will battle the predators with their own resources. Even as I drove away from campus and would not be there with him, I was there. I chanted words of wisdom to myself and whispered them aloud so Noel could hear them. Trust. Release. Trust. Release.

So too is Jesus's relationship with us. Jesus walks with us, believes in us and has equipped us to battle our predators. He loves us, has plans to prosper us. Because He is not here does not mean He is not there. Read that again. It's worth it.

Because Welly was with me in this car driving down the mountain did not mean she was not there. Welly's spirit and love was never *not* there with her boy in his land.

Matthew 28:20 (NKJV)
...I am with you always, even to the end of the age.

Step #25

Be in the Be

O N A COLORADO WINTER DAY, it is common practice to open the front door of our home to let the high-altitude, blue-sky presence slip through the glass door. This ritual in our home, be it warm or cold outside, awakens hope and sprinkles promise into the space. The morning sun shows itself in majestic rays through the glass pane with its so-close-to-the-sun dance. In that moment, breath returns, a day I have not seen before appears, and nature pours upon the well-worn rug. Worn Rug invites a presence to come. Sit. To soak up the potential of good and fair and just. Birds flit by the front door as they scurry to drink from the bath placed just so. The boards in the wooden floor expand and contract and expand. And, in their movement, they speak. The invitation comes. Come. Be in the Be.

Because Noel was always dignified and proud and awe-struck by the simple, she watched the whole thing unfold each morning from afar, at first. Out of one side-eye, she watched the door open and the sun fall upon the rug, and she heard the floorboards sigh. Vitamin D was to be had. Heat therapy for sore joints awaited. It was not until the proper invitation was offered that she'd take her place upon the rug. Noel knew rituals provided safety in our moments of transition and in all of our days. She knew protocols and would not show up had she not been invited.

With a higher than necessary pitch, raised eyebrows, and the enthusiasm of a child, I spoke the invitation. "Ah-Welly. S-Uh-shine." She knew in this ritual her role was to first forgive me once again for the ridiculousness of using words that were not real. Then, she would saunter nearer from her hunting spot on the ottoman. She would meander by, purposefully wag her two-inch tail at slow-motion speed, and intentionally place her belly upon the rug as if she was a practicing yoga guru with grace and ease. With back legs extended upon the weathered rug, she would settle in to soak up some of that free S-Uh-shine.

The more she accepted the invitation, the more she modeled self-care. The more she demonstrated being open and willing to receive in this moment, the more she demonstrated to me the fruition of faith. In just fifteen minutes in the S-Uh-shine without a book or a podcast, the voice of grace arrives. Sitting with no life-noise can be scary, I discovered. All the stinkin' weight of all those dimes I am carrying around surface in this quiet space and in this place. Here, I can access my current awareness and begin the arduous, intentional work of facing some truths related to my current state of being.

After many sessions of S-Uh-shine, I came to believe that when we are open, present, and willing, we invite holy. Holy wisdom comes in the simple, and for me that is where knowingness surfaces. I believe the S-Uh-shine ritual began to teach me that when I allow myself permission to lay in the mess for a bit, rolling around in the dusty fibers of life, structure comes. Even in the middle of what can feel like pure chaos.

Many times as Noel S-Uh-shined, I sat with her. I allowed my eyes to slit into half-moons like Ah-Well's as the sun's rays penetrated our skin and seeped into our muscles, our spines, and our beings. On Worn Rug, I smelled Ah-Well's warm sun-shiny breath and watched her belly expand and contract. Noel was meditating and had stepped away from predator protect-ing. Her punched-in and on-the-clock approach to keeping mice, prairie dogs, deer, stupid darkness, fear, and anxiety away was retired when simply Being in the Be. Restoration. Restoration right here, right now. Upon the worn rug.

In this moment of rug meditation, she affirmed to herself, *I belong*. I imagined her speaking to her heart and her mind in the tiny hush of each moment that occurred between the bird's flutter of their wings. In this rug moment, Noel whis-pered wisdom-words to herself: *Valuable, capable, able, seen, loved.*

I recall thinking as I sat with her that maybe Jesus came to my home in the form of an old rug. No. However, what I confidently profess, is that these Being-in-the-Be moments require no dimes, no coupons, and are, in fact, entirely free. I envisioned dimes falling out of my pockets, my heart, and my hands. While Noel spoke love to herself, I practiced. I practiced embracing the idea of really surrendering. How wild it was to let it be.

My practice of letting go of dimes and envisioning the new had to continue. Unlike Noel, I had to fight to keep the old tapes from running around in my mind. It's stinkin' hard to break old habits. In my meditating head, I heard snake hisses, work conversations, middle-aged sighs, financial data, and insurance woes. Holy Toledo. These predators in this poorly rated film were clouding my stinkin' Holy. Clearly, I was going to benefit from more practice time. These new ways required commitment from me and faith in myself to liberate into the next season.

How had Welly, on this rug, so easily surrendered her trinity self of mind, body, and spirit to be enveloped in a cloak of something bigger in just a matter of a few deep sighs? Did she know something I had forgotten? Could it be this simple? I coached myself. Yes, dumping the dimes and leaving my work to a bigger entity for a sacred moment is how I would realign, refuel, re-examine, and reflect. Just like Welly. Yes, just like Noel.

In hindsight, I see that my evolution was a result of using Noel as a model and tapping into faith in myself and my knowingness of where it came from. It came from quiet private moments with a four-legged friend who arrived unexpectedly. It came from permission I granted myself to accept my role in this place called Earth. It came from predators and breaking the necks of resentment, regret, and betrayal. It came in recognition of the ebb and flow, the falling apart and coming back together.

Befriending the need to be born again in a new story that *I* would create validated that *I* would become a part of the natural order of things. Willingness to take charge to grow came from gut-wrenching, never-goes-away-only-shifts grief. It all arrived from soaking up tiny moments of purposeful awe-finding in each day's walk. This thing named Evolutionary

Spirit came from Worn Rug in that holy space. It came without words.

Noel grabbed S-Uh-shine moments often. She was quick to surrender among trees in a valley or upon rocks at water's side. She would bask with slit eyes on a beach and at a pier by the reservoir, enjoying its cool breeze. When she sat alone in these moments, she was never alone. She was with the breeze and it with her. She was with her boy among blades of summer grass.

Jesus, just like Noel, is self-care. Self-care opportunities are here. Self-care is available in the inhale of my breath or upon an old rug anytime. No need to run, strive, struggle, and search. Being-in-the-Be is what brings the gentle, wise, internal voice of reason that says, *"Let's go this way now."*

Isaiah 30:21 (ESV)
And your ears shall hear a word behind you,
saying, "This is the way, walk in it," when you
turn to the right or when you turn to the left.

Step #26

Surrender. Liberate.

M Y CAR WAS NOEL'S CAR. As soon as we started moving she would place her muscle-bound self in the front seat, her ears on high alert, her purple collar sloppily flung upon her neck, and her right paw on the window. She would give me the side-eye as a way of impressing upon me this was not a sing-to-the-radio-time or chat time. This is business, and we have a lot of ground to cover at such fast speeds. As it was with the knuckle-head musicians in The Blues Brothers, we were on a mission from God. Or were we?

During the dog days of summer, while Noel's boy was working his way through his first two years of transcendence in various college classes, Noel and I would run errands around town together. One summer day, at twenty-five seconds into the red light at a four-way, congested intersection, I sensed Noel's head do the hyper-focus head turn. Before I could cast my gaze in her direction to see what had averted her attention, she jumped out of the barely opened window. How she managed to squeeze her body through the small opening I will never know. Perhaps she had learned a thing or two from those snakes. Ewe. Like lightning, she sprinted to the prairie dog who was now-screeching warning calls to the family. In the time it took me to cuss seven times, the light to change to green, and the chump next to me to yell, "Hey lady, your dog is catching that thing!" she had, indeed. I know! I know! Yes, she had indeed broke its…I won't finish.

Somehow in my mass hysteria, I managed to pull away from the intersection, release my seatbelt, and turn on my hazard lights. Oh my, the looks of the passersby. Drivers' heads were shaking back and forth. If my lip-reading skills served me, I saw one set mouth, "My God, lady. How?"

I stomped my way to Noel in the field where she stood upon the deceased, and the closer I came, the more her tail wagged until she sloppily plopped her bottom upon the earth. Our eyes met, she panted and gave me that ears-back smile. Without restraint I stood above her, hands on hips. "Welly! Now get in the car. You've GOT to stop killing things."

We both scooted quickly to the capsule and hopped in with heads hung low, basked in shame. We drove home with the radio gently playing in the background. I chose. The two of us drug ourselves into our living room. I sat upon the floor. She sat in front of me still uttering a fake pant here and there. We looked at each other and I began.

"Father God, please forgive us. That whole scene was quite humiliating and dangerous and, quite honestly, pretty gross and sad. So stinkin' sad. We really do love all your creatures, except maybe one, but you know that, and we both feel super, super bad about how this transpired. Please forgive me for leaving the window open, and please forgive Noel for breaking…well, you know."

Then, as hands of warmth seemed to have enveloped us both, Noel plopped herself on her side upon the carpet and her head on my crisscrossed legs as if to remind us both that what we really needed was some S-Uh-shine. We needed to breathe in that S-Uh-shine space, and in it, we both were reminded—He has it.

He has it even though we can't see it. We must have faith that He has the prairie dog right now. Because of His love and unwavering protection, He has the prairie dog, and we were graced forgiveness. His ultimate will, although in chaotic circumstances, was still completed. He has the creature that was seen as a potential predator to the domesticated dog. I suppose, He had Teenager and me too in this wild season of wandering on a sometimes winding trail.

In our rug repentance, I re-learned, He has us dogs. The two right here: me and Noelly. Perhaps more importantly, in the S-Uh-shine space of the Be, we realized we could leave behind so many of those predators that threaten us in our daily walk. He's got them too. We could surrender.

In this moment of shame, I used what I had been practicing; I whispered, "I am clean. I am renewed. I am moving toward the next. I am evolving." As I whispered, I envisioned myself behind my closed eyelids. Me. Surrounded in the knowingness that it's all gonna be okay.

This realization that I had already begun to step into my new season was liberating. I did not have to ward off predators. I did not have to leave behind all of me to walk into a new piece of my spectacular life. I could cling to the dandelion-tying, rock-painting little girl inside of me. I could drop all the old dimes and replace them with parts of my soul that needed a good dusting off. Those parts were calling my name. Noelly and I could take one deep yoga downward dog pose followed by a lion's breath exhale of relief. Now we could fully enjoy S-Uh-shing together.

I thought I'd hung up that old dishtowel some time ago, but it wasn't until this moment in my life story that I really shook off some of the heaviest weight. I started to surrender some of the anxiety that woke me up at 2:00 a.m. Anxiety about things that were not in my control. Thank goodness! Fretting over loved ones' safety and choices. Fretting over the last thing I did not say to the one friend I had one time. She and I walked so many miles in our town that a new residential home development salesperson recognized us, asked about where to camp and picnic and inquired about the locale of the streets we strolled. That friend got lots of my fretting energy for neglecting to say a million and two things before her last breath. My tears did not let my lips work as she breathed in. You know. I know you know. I fretted over the boss's words and expertly made them into a horror movie by 2:20 a.m.

Son had a friend way back in the Baby Snuggles era. Colorado fifth graders were given a free ski pass each year. Now, who sat at that conference table to create this ingenious plan? Was it for the ski industry to address sustainability? Some folks were creating their futures in the ski mecca, which is a much better conference-table decision than having me memorizing PLU numbers to ring up my own oranges and avocados at the checkout counter.

Fifth-grade son invited Matty to ski with us. Long ceremony for Matty's name. Matt was just too, too much for sweet, hilarious, sensitive Matty. In response to the invitation, Matty replied, "No thanks. I have fraids."

"Fraids?" I asked.

"Yes, I'm fraid of skiing and fraid of Halloween and stuff."

OH! Fraids. Some name fraids anxiety, predators, or dimes. Yes, Matty, fraids.

As we mature in *our house*, we can walk in faith, knowing that while we regroup, re-energize, rejoice in our own life, He is there, helping to keep the predators away. In self-care moments, we can be the dog with huge ears and little, sweet paws who loves S-Uh-shine. We can surrender the angst. We can lay in sanctuary space where peace, a future, and knowingness take control. In that moment of space, we can take that work stress, family conflict, stench from aggressive snakes, uncertainty, and middle-aged blahs and break their necks.

In the sanctuary of S-Uh-shine, we give away our fraids.

Psalm 55:22 (NLV)
Give all your cares to the Lord and
He will give you strength.

Step #27

Speak

"I come from creative survivors." "I'm transcending." "It's okay." Mantras and word phrases were splashed on sticky notes. My mantra sticky notes by my toothbrush were splattered with paste and spittle. "My job proposal will knock their socks off." That one took two sticky notes and hung on my dashboard. "I craft my path." "I am what I am looking for." Hung on my mirror in my yoga room. "Rug repentance rules!" Hung on my daily calendar. With Teenager's absence in these two years at college, I found the bitter-sweet flutter of his wings had afforded me focus. I put details in the job proposal. I worked to draft a budget and included short- and long-term vision descriptions. In this proposal was my voice, and it was about to be shared in a conference room where I would sit with others. My voice would be present in this space with no PLU numbers. *I have a voice. Look at me, Marge.*

Welly was the poster child for work-life balance. Again and again, I witnessed Noel's unwavering strength in her mission to protect, teach, work, play, model, and be of service. There were never enough walks, runs through the field, or five-mile hikes to squelch Noel's need to explore and compete against herself, and she rarely punched out. Her calling from within was so directly aligned with the things she loved.

Seems like moons and moons ago when Teenager was still in high school. One moons-ago Friday evening, I was winding down after an extraordinarily challenging day at work. I walked into the room where my son's high school friends gathered. I observed Noel gravitating toward the rowdy bunch. When socializing with Teenager and his testosterone-filled tribe, Noelly remained on the clock while magically alternating from this lap to that one as she soaked up deep-voiced kisses. She was beloved by Teenager's friends, and in addition to yelling, "Hi, Noel!" as they drove past us in their rusty cars with windows down, she often had visits throughout the weekdays.

If class was canceled at the local high school…wait, do high school classes get canceled? Hmm. Anyway, when class was "canceled," the whole lot of them would show up to escort Noel to the backyard. Noel recognized teenaged shenanigans but never spoke a word. Why would she? Being the center of attention from a group of jovial, handsome teens was evidence of her otherworldly magnetism. Receiving cuddles, playing a bit of ball, and rolling around in muscle-bound arms was when the word *clan* was defined for her. Noel could monitor the property, catch a ball, do zoomies, and give kisses all in one breath. She was part of their pack, and without skipping a beat, she masterfully balanced her work and her life calling. Noel's use of her authentic self *was* her work. I remember studying her and began to believe that if I paused long enough, I also could begin reinventing what *work* looked like for me in this new stage of life. *There's the intentional crafting of my life*, I thought.

The apostles, Jesus's rag-tag group of young men, had to pause when Jesus asked for their support. They may have even rolled their eyes as they considered the outlandish request from Jesus to transition into new roles, new behaviors, and new work. I imagine, they might have felt a bit fed up with the entire situation too. A bit fed up with the way things were going for them. Fed up with their jobs and relationships, and fed up with their past hopes for their dreams of what they thought their futures would be. They had to be exhausted from walking the treadmill, doing what everyone else did, falling into the drama of the talk on the streets.

The story goes that once they heeded the call and left all the old fish nets behind, they were shown the way, and purpose-filled living returned in new form. Stunning. And sweet. And miraculous, really.

There were few things that would cause Welly to roll her eyes. Wearing a pink collar, watching TV, and socializing with a neighbor's pet were absolute, solid, hard passes. After all, this was a very short life, and she would not waste the time she had. Noel knew we were to love our neighbors. That concept, right there, was perhaps one of her greatest, most agonizing struggles and caused the most eye rolling.

In enters Blessings. I still crave a moment of invisible presence when Blessings's naming ceremony took place. Blessings was a curly, snow-white, highly manicured miniature poodle who never walked fast enough to create tension on any leash. She had a perfectly round face that highlighted her tiny coalblack eyes. Blessings was the postcard dog, and she was the neighbor. Noel spent hours and days that eventually morphed into years watching Blessings prance upon the sidewalk right in front of our front yard viewing window.

On the other paw, Noel loved watching mail carriers and would give them all the tiniest of tail wag from her perch each day. She had determined, based on their consistent but odd behavior, that they were not a predator. These carriers of paper were obsessed with the box. On summer afternoons, she would sit on the front stoop and raise her head toward them as they placed the mail in the box container. She had observed the "What's sup, dude" nod from her boy-clan hundreds of times and greeted our hipster mail carrier in a similar fashion. Noel adored the front window and loved working that post.

On one particular extraordinary day, Welly's entire human pack left. They were to be gone for a few consecutive days. During Welly's pack's absence, she got to have a visitor. We named her The Visitor because Noel would have rolled her eyes to infinity and beyond if we referred to The Visitor as a pet sitter.

The story goes that as soon as the leash was fastened, Noel began wagging her tail and jumping in place in celebration of their impending adventure. As Noel and The Visitor walked through the garage door to exit the house, there in the drive-way was Blessings. Now that's something to think about, isn't it? Blessings entering when they least expected it. Ain't that the truth?

Upon seeing Blessings, Noel stopped on a dime. Clearly, this was a dime Noel had been clinging to for years. Blessings was prancing about on Noel's driveway with those painted nails and diamond collar sparkling in the sun. When a laser beam from one of her diamonds pierced Noel's eye, she approached Blessings and gave her a scolding that would cause any kid in overalls back on the farm to drop their pail of water and stand in stunned silence.

The Visitor reported that Noel's mouth was almost touching Blessings's right ear during the scolding, and Noel really laid it on her. Noel bark-talked her for an earth-shattering few seconds until Blessings's owner yelled something like, "In Heaven's name, no!" and proceeded to pick up Blessings and remove her from the scene.

How many years had Noel waited? Of all days, and with her pack gone, why was this the day Blessings ventured onto the driveway? Apparently, it was simply *the* day. Maybe Blessings really did arrive in times when Noel needed it most.

To Blessings, Noel spoke.

"Listen, don't mess with this house, this driveway, or The Visitor, and certainly don't be coming up in here in your curly groomed head and your little diamonds when my pack is gone. Don't be prancing by this house anymore as if to say you are an elite member of society and you're not obligated to provide any service except for sitting pretty in photos. Don't you tinkle your toes anymore upon this space or this cul-de-sac. If you're going to attempt to reign over us servants, us broken, us in need, us fallible beings, then go do it over there on your hill, and let Jesus do His work here."

Now I am not a trained dog whisperer, but after watching Noel do Noel for years and watching Blessings tippy toe by each day, I'm pretty sure that it was a dime Welly was hanging on to. She just needed the right time to approach the subject, say her piece, and purge that angst forever more.

Perhaps our absence created a sanctuary moment for Welly. Perhaps in that quiet, she too, became reflective. Perhaps she began to experience a bit of a wandering spirit, a sense of loss, and anxiety about the future. Perhaps she knew it was time to take inventory of her dimes and recognized it may be time for a purge. Time to release baggage she was holding on to in preparation for her new path. Maybe it was time for her to settle grievances and to clear a space in her soul for new to enter.

Stunning, really. Noel didn't lay a finger or a paw on Blessings. She literally put her mouth to Blessings's ear, which as you know is ever so close to her n-e-c-k. When we arrived home, Visitor told us the story, and for some unknown reason, we never saw Blessings and her owner prance by the front window again.

Jesus sort of did what Welly did with those who had positional power back in the day. The kings really did not want to hear what Jesus had to say in the gatherings He hosted upon many of the hillsides. The kings pranced around in their fancy-pants attire and commanded, directed, and shunned the common folks' voice. When Jesus appeared in his tattered clothes, the pharaohs and kings could not conceive Jesus had much to say about eternal life or being saved and forgiven from the stupid things we do daily and love. They couldn't see, or rather, weren't brave enough to invest in seeing the power in Jesus's words and presence. Until, of course, Jesus firmly approached their right ear and spoke truth to them. "I am the way, the truth, and the light."

In those words, and after performing countless healings and miracles, he certainly piqued the Pharisees' interest, at least.

Welly wasn't proclaiming in Blessings's ear that she was the Savior, but I do believe she was preaching the Word. She spoke of contributing to the effort of universal love, however that looked for Blessings. She spoke of living in the mind frame of humble ways and acceptance, forgiveness, and servanthood. She scold-reminded everyone in that driveway that we are all broken, including Welly. Including diamond-clad Blessings. That brokenness in us is what unites us as humans. Or dogs. Or both.

I wonder if Noel had to ask for a bit of forgiveness after preaching to Blessings. After all, maybe that was indeed Blessings's calling, to prance around and get her nails painted. And, maybe, just maybe, Welly was being a little judgy. Regardless, Noel was able to shed that dime she'd carried for far too long. She took that pent-up angst to the driveway and broke its neck. Now, her pockets have room for acorns and sticks and bunny fur she finds in tufts on the forest bed.

Standing up for what is right is work. I know this intimately as a female young leader in my preacher-kid home and later in the world of work. As a preacher's kid, I saw too many women with black eyes and shaken-trauma teens enter our home as Dad escorted them into our den—a safe place to hide from the predators that were in their homes and their bedrooms. I saw my parents hand over my piggy bank on too many occasions to count to couples who sat at our dining room table with tears floating in the man's eyes. They spoke languages I did not recognize. I served home-grown tomato juice as an appetizer to all the addicted, lonely, widowed, recently released prisoners on Thanksgiving at our kitchen table. We sat among them as Dad welcomed them into our safe home. I heard the brutal truth being spoken at all of those tables in hushed whispers. "She can't stay there." "They need to leave Chicago immediately." "All we serve here is Libby's home-canned tomato juice during this holiday. Your addiction is safe here."

As school administrator, I found myself being the one who had to say *it* aloud. "We could have shooters walk in this door." "Your child is struggling." "There is another mandate to meet without additional resources."

My family never, ever had a holiday without humanity being present. The two Muds cleaned, served, and sat quietly around the bonfire that blazed on each one of our tables in our home. The Muds were quick to share that this life was a lot of stinkin' work as we lamented about not having "normal" Christmas morning or a "regular" Thanksgiving dinner. We gained a reputation among our peer groups for being "those girls who never have a Santa pop by" or "the girls who have the family where strangers come to dinner." In hindsight, I suppose, we were the ones doing the right thing. Right. The right thing, even though it gave us quite the reputation. Noel too gained a reputation after her Blessings incident within a few particular cul-de-sac homes.

Hearing of Noel's scolding-of-the-Blessings, I promised to bring Noel's story into my life as a model. That thing that Noel did. That thing that occurred on our driveway was Noel's preacher's voice, speaking her truth. What an act of self-love. Sometimes, when we are attempting to become the being we must become, we bravely tap into our preacher's voice even if it taints our reputation a bit. Sacrificing my reputation for the right side of right is always right. I saw that, even for Noel, some days were just a bit more extraordinarily challenging. Me too, Welly. Me too.

Just as the oak tree shimmers in the fall breeze, the three of us—son, me, and Well-Well—stood in our respective forests of life. There were tangible signs we three magi were transcending. I could put my pointer finger out past my hand and touch the moment I had begun to reap the rewards of the work I put into the process of my personal change. That day Noel and I drove home after visiting the boy in his mountain town, that. I point to the collective sigh and see I was able to release him a bit easier than the time before. Those sticky notes shaping my new thinking and forming new tapes in my head to replace the parent tapes of old, that. That daisy necklace sitting on my passenger seat, that. That impact-the-world job proposal I had finally submitted, that. All of those things I could point to were the *that's* that were transforming me. Those *that's* were revised and were the much more weathered but wiser me. And to think, all the ordinary and mundaneness in each act was coming from my shifting soul's code. Perhaps the most startling *that* of all the *that's* was an invitation to keynote a room of people with pockets full of money just waiting to spend on teenagers in our community who needed a place to be seen and heard. This fundraiser event was expecting just over eight hundred people. When I received the invite to be the keynote speaker at the occasion, I wrote another sticky note. "Hey, Mr. Randy, I'm a speaker." Then I dropped the mic and the dime

and walked out of that story. Walked right out of that story.
Truth.

Ephesians 4:15 (ISV)
Instead, by speaking the truth in love,
we will grow up completely...

Step #28

Believe You Will Stand Again and Again and Again

ONE PARTICULAR FALL DAY, WHEN Noel was very young, we went for a sidewalk jaunt. What a joy to watch her bounce in her own being, thrilled to be out with the trees, the cars, and with the bugs meandering along the path. On this day, she wandered off to the side of the path, extending the leash way beyond my personal space. She grabbed a rock and cradled the stone in her mouth. She backtracked her steps to face me. She stood directly in front of me with rock in mouth. She threw the rock in the air landing it right at my feet. I kicked the rock, it rolled ahead. Noel then ran ahead, picked it up in her mouth, and returned it to me by flinging it out of her mouth so that it would land near my feet. This back and forth running added steps to her daily walk. This game we named Rock. When we would leash-walk years after the creation of this first game, I would look at her and say, "Rock?" She would immediately seek a rock and the game began. Again.

Noel knew how to throw a little sacred into each walk, each day, and each moment. She knew how to take what seemed like a fair day and improve it tenfold. She used her break-its-neck technique to grab the rock and fling it up into the air like she did with the prairie dog—oh, dang. We were not to mention that again. We had been forgiven. We don't have to dwell anymore inside of that dog-gone story.

She used her work skills and her staving-off-predator skills even when playing. If that's not work-life balance, I don't know what it is. How easy it is to place the dishtowel again upon my chest when I am work weary and put my head to the grindstone to just plod along. Reinventing a new vision of balancing work with life and taking responsibility to turn the fair day into extraordinary takes work. Watching Welly find the play within the work. Noel was miraculously inspiring. She was. Dog-gone, she was! This intentional act of finding true balance between work and play is an act I can and will bring into my daily walk, even while I waited to hear about my job proposal I had submitted and presented for review. No putting my eggs all in one basket anymore. No expectations from the folks that would be considering my proposal. No. Instead, I now practice using my evolutionary tools to evolve even if I am required to stay where I am. I can do this thing named Work. I have a rock, somewhere, to play with at work. I'm taking responsibility. Just like Welly. Yes. Play at work. Yes.

I was stinkin' pleased with my proposal and was sitting in waiting to hear if it took with the higher-ups. If I may, I say I was starting to do quite well in these intentional evolutionary efforts as of late. In accessing my work-life balance, I knew I first must define the current state of my workday and cull the pieces of each part of my day apart. This process, I imagined, would serve as an accountability piece for me later down my never-before-walked path.

There was waking up and preparing for the day of work, the salaried work. There was driving to work and being at work. There was the coming home part, so I could do more work at home. You know…chores, addressing clogged toilets, paying bills, exercise class, relating to all the people. You know the people. The people in the house and in the neighborhood, the store, the plumber, the people. All the parts of my day were work. Until. Until I put the dishes to the side one day after a game of Rock and paused. Instead of answering those timebound emails and scrubbing that burnt spaghetti sauce-pan, I dug through an old box of pictures of the girl with her dreams and silly helium parts who is now resurfacing. I saw a girl dressed like a flapper for Halloween (what the heck kind of costume was that?), and I recalled what I liked best about that attire was the costume jewelry. Hey, where is that jewelry? I saw a girl squatting in the park picking enormous bouquets of dandelions. I saw a book of poems written by a third grader and a tiny girl in her favorite hoodie sweatshirt sitting alone on a fishing pier with her feet dangling in the fish bubbles. I saw a girl with water-colored painted rocks in her hands. I saw me. Me. Playing.

Peering backwards, I saw me as a girl, a teen, an adult, a professional, and finally a snake wrangler. I accepted my truth. There was so much sacred joy in those seasons. Sure, there were times I was gored by words I let penetrate me, stall me, put me in bed for a day or two. But I could still smell those fish bubbles wafting off the water's gentle wave. I could feel those tube-like dandelion stems in between each finger. When I walked, just like Welly, through my day, I too could grab ahold of a rock and throw that which gives me joy into any day. I too can allow time each day for a bit of Rock game, a bit of painting, or the weaving of daisies. I could sink my teeth into self-made joy by busting out the old ways in new form.

After years of playing Rock, Noelly's dentist was required to remove her six front teeth. After surgery, grabbing snakes, squished bunny toys, and rocks became a feat of tremendous skill. She had to strategically and gingerly place everything to the side of her mouth. The side bite was no deterrent, but she was forever altered.

And me? I was keeping my teeth but started to shed my corporate-climber identity, my mom-of-a-little-boy title, and the role of a daughter with parents on Earth. I dug my teeth into daily agendas that included time to color and weave potholders again on one of those craft store plastic looms. I began to speak more frequently to my angels, since it seemed I had many now. I let go of wishing dead people would talk to me and instead began to trust more in the knowingness. The knowingness that the divine speaks and leads and guides and comforts in ways that are unexplained by mere words. The same divine love and guidance I had as a little girl painting pebbles was the same love that helped me to transcend into yet another season of life. In a metaphorical way, I suppose, I too was losing teeth. Teeth that used to clench on to old. Noel and I shed a bit of our life naivety. We were no longer so idealistic, but we were becoming wiser.

I watched Welly adapt and transform with her side bite. She displayed great prowess, flexibility, and fortitude in her metamorphosis. I released my tightened jaw and let my teeth separate. With the release of my clenched approach, I created space and made more room in my mouth to speak a new story. I swear, I saw a dime fall from my lips as my jaw relaxed into its home.

I watched Noel enjoy the dropping of a few dimes as well to create space for what was to enter in her final season. Things had changed around her, yet her name was still written in her boy's life and in Jesus's. She was still called to protect, inspire, teach.

Noel did occasionally suffer in the sanctuary place of the in-between. Her missing teeth, her speed, and ability to judge how fast and how hard to run seemed to land her in a bit of a mess occasionally. Sanctuary time is not always pretty.

Once, there was a bunny that ran across Main Street. Noel pulled so hard on her leash, she escaped my grip and got clipped by a car. Once, there was a bear that crept into our backyard at 4:00 a.m. Noel ran through her doggie door to go tell that bear that we were sleeping and that bear had better leave. She scolded the bear right up a tree. Literally. By the time I got outside to get her into the house, the neighbors were not happy. Her barking had awakened them. Imagine that. As a seasoned dog, neighbors held her to high standards in decision-making. Scolding bears in the wee hours of the morning tainted her reputation, again. Going from carefree to wise was a messy and muddy place and a muddy process.

One chilly fall day, during rutting season, Noel was gored and flung across the property by a twelve-point buck while she was protecting our backyard. Afterward, she lay absolutely still in her bed for seventy-two hours, allowing the puncture wound to ooze and release the pain. I brought her water and spooned it into her mouth between belabored breaths. She sat in S-Uh-shine and prayed and rested and held to her faith that the great healer would provide. I remember longing for Noel's boy and wishing he was present. At the time of her goring, her boy was hiking New Zealand and felt very, very far away. He was seeking himself in the mountains, and I told Noel as she lay resting that I would try to get her boy on the phone. I would place the phone near her ear, I explained, and the two could speak. On the second day of her lying in her bed, my son came off the mountain and all the two of us could mutter was "Oh no. Oh no." Tears for the fear, tears for the missing. Tears for the separation and tears for hoped-for healing. Oh no.

Somewhere in the seventy-third hour, she stood on wobbly legs. She was carried to the grass and cradled back to her resting place. I cleaned her puncture wound and, with tears running down my face, thanked her for her sacrifice. In her ear, I whispered the story of puncture wounds in the hands and feet of Jesus while I gently caressed her side body. On the third night, Noel stood again. She shuffled to her food bowl. Take and eat. She did.

Noel was persecuted, shunned by the locals, and gored. However, she never lost sight of who she was at her core. As her days and years passed, she heeded her call, stayed steady, saw the awe in each day, morphed, and transformed season after season. So many didn't understand and didn't recognize all she did was in preparation for her next radical inward transformation. Her story sounds a little bit like a man in rag-tag sandals who came to transition and ascend before our very eyes.

Where Lost is Found

Romans 5:3–4 (NIV)

...but we also glory in our sufferings, because we know that suffering produces perseverance; perseverance, character; and character, hope.

Step #29

Let Your Angels Enter

WE NEVER STOPPED CELEBRATING NOEL'S miraculous recovery. We continued to live!

It was a Colorado-bluebird-sky kind of day, and with wild abandonment, we grabbed our swim gear and rafting shoes and headed out. I know for certain Welly had core memories deep within her soul of spending past days on the river with her boy when he was in high school and college. In my heart, I now pictured him in foreign lands, and perhaps he was floating on another river with Welly in his heart.

Well-Well squinted her eyes as she counted the steps of our packing routine. The last few items were placed in my adventure bag, and finally, we grabbed the water bottles and sunscreen. It was her turn. I gave her the nod, and she hopped in the car. We caressed every curve of the mountain path, listening to the lazy river dance along the highway.

There's something to be said about leaving behind the typical daily walk to join an entirely new community of trees, fish, bugs, and rocks. There's something to be said about recognizing all that gives me joy. When I know what brings me joy, I can be intentional about bringing it back into my life any time I need. When I open my senses and allow them to speak to me, I hear better, I see better, and I know everything better. Stinky old tire tubes and their silky sides rubbing on my summer legs pleases my nose and surfaces memories of connections long gone, tears of unleashed laughter with childhood friends, and risk-free adventures that had for so many days colored my youth and flooded my soul.

We had arrived. Our small floating community placed the tubes into the four-inch water. Bottoms began to occasionally scrape a rock in the ridiculously safe shallow waters. Our group was off for a few hours of peace-filled summer fun. Just the way Welly likes it. As we slipped through the shallow waters, Noel hopped into one tube, walked across the shallow water, and hopped onto another lap. At one point, we all felt the waters deepen a bit. Before we could talk about the quickening water, Noel jumped into my tube and sat on top of my sinking lap. The speed at which we moved down the river quickly accelerated. Our group separated, some being pulled this way and others that.

Suddenly, Noel and I found ourselves preparing for a head-on collision with a tree that had fallen into the rushing creek years ago. The force at which my feet met the log buckled my knees and flipped the front of the tube up and over our heads, plunging us upside down into the rushing water. I recall doing what felt like a somersault under the tumultuous water before becoming pinned under the fallen tree. I was unable to escape or stand. In my bent over position, head and body fully immersed in the rushing waters, I could feel the tree limb lying upon my back and the current pushing upon my bottom and calves. There was a conscience moment when I realized Noel was not under the water with me. By God's grace and angels' heavy hands, my feet were pushed out from under me. With a great force upon my back, I then was released out from beneath the grip of the tree's limb. My head surfaced. I gasped for a breath. My shoes were gone. The tube was gone. Noel was gone.

After having been whisked some three hundred feet downstream, my feet grasped the water's bed for footing. The water calmed and I stood. I shook my head back and forth, rubbed my eyes. Had I thrown Noel out of the tube before hitting the tree limb? Yes, I had. I knew she was a swimmer, and if she could be free from the tree limb, she would swim to the side of the mountain. A pair of tubers passed by me as I stood in the water's rush. They spoke with panic in their voice. They, too, had been taken off guard at the unexpected force of the water.

"Your dog! We grabbed him but had to throw him. We threw him onto the bank." Then they were swept away.

Him, I thought.

The water caressed every curve of my toes, my ankles, and shins. Me and Jesus standing in the midst of Mother Nature. Me knowing I had made the biggest mistake of the decade. I had forgotten what I knew.

Colorado rivers are sweet and lazy until they are not. I knew this. But in the temptation to float in a four-inch stream, with hopes of bringing back a time in my life that was never coming back, I accepted the invitation. Sometimes, temptation comes in the form of ignoring what we know.

I got my body to the river's edge and was able to claw my way up a few feet of the mountain's slope. My brain had gone limbic: completely incapable of emotional processing. All I was sure of was that I had thrown Noel away. I stood in the middle of mountain pinecones and could not see her or hear her. In an attempt to save her, I transitioned on a dime in those tumultuous waters to fulfill the role of protector. In that river, our roles were reversed. My angels could enter when I was most vulnerable and surrendered control. Two angel wings and my shaky arms protected Ah-Well from a predator.

I hollered her name. I squinted my ears to hear rustling in the pine trees. I placed my hands around my mouth to make a megaphone and whistled. I yelled her many names with tears welling in my eyes. Suddenly, I heard branches crackle, and out of the pinecone-dusted mountainside, she appeared. Smiling, tail wagging, and panting. Drenched and dirty, she was there.

How we returned to the parking area is not this story. This story is about abandonment, forgiveness, and grace. It's about small miracles and angels on tubes in waters not for man. This story is about dimes and a boy-turned-man, an otherworldly presence, and light entering into a space that was feeling a little gloomy-ish, and snakes too.

After a few days of sitting with my I-almost-drowned story, I somehow made peace with this narrative by forgiving myself for the trauma my reckless tubing choice had created. Although throwing Noel to the raging waters was the right thing to do when facing an impending collision with a tree, it was only in my faith I could do that. I had to know that sometimes we have to abandon things we believe we have control around and let the angels come in. And boy howdy, did they. Those angels scooped Noel up and threw "him" to the curb.

Psalm 91:11–12 (ISV)
For he will command his angels to protect you in all your ways. With their hands they will lift you up so you will not trip over a stone.

Step #30

While Snacking on Pig Food, Allow Grace to Enter

ALMOST-YOUNG-MAN'S CALLING TOOK HIM AWAY. Away from the confines of what used to be considered his home. Away from the local pizza joint and friends from childhood and streets he walked and biked and eventually drove for years. Away from middle-aged angsty mom questioning him about life plans. Away from the known and away from what became, for him, the old.

Almost-Young-Man's given name started to show its direct connection to his ancestor's lineage. He heard the calling to wander, explore, and hike foreign mountains. Almost-Young-Man traveled with a backpack and a girl named Friend to Thailand, New Zealand, Europe, the island of Borneo, and more. They picked apples to earn enough pocket money to hike the next mountain. They lived in cars and hostels and under the stars. Almost-Young-Man was gone from my home more than not. I sat in the Be and chatted with Noel about who the three of us were becoming in our next season of life.

A parable in the Bible tells of a boy named Prodigal Son. He had two names. Prodigal and Son. This son asked for and received his father's inheritance, got it, then squandered it away. Apparently, Prodigal Son lived a life of indulgence and was reckless with the fortune his father had given him. Gosh, Prodigal Son. Well, I never!

After he was left with nothing, it became necessary for him to work as a hired hand. As he was feeding the pigs one day, he got so hungry (yes, literally and figuratively, of course) that he considered eating the pigs' food. Prodigal Son had gone from riches to poverty and found himself in the middle. The in-between. At this lowest of low points in his life, he returned to his father's home to ask for forgiveness and hoped to gain employment as a servant on his very own father's farm.

His father welcomed Prodigal Son's return with open arms, and—get this—his father hosted a party in honor of his return. The brother who had remained loyal and hard-working during Prodigal Son's absence was not happy about this scene. I can imagine that when the loyal son had to witness their father throwing a party for Prodigal Son who squandered his good fortune and abandoned his family, he wanted to take his brother, give him a good shake like Noel did with those over-whelming charged emotions. You know, break-its-neck kind of release. Break its neck.

When Prodigal Son returned, his father looked at the elder son and kind of said something like, "Hey, listen. We celebrate his coming home and that's that." You and I know Dad did not mean his coming home in a literal sense. Home. Home to who he was called to be by God. Home to his authentic, broken, and so deeply loved and forgiven amazing self. Home to God's voice within him.

As Almost-Young-Man toured the world, Noel waited. There was no judgement, no harbored anger. Welly had faith. He would come again onto her porch, into her home. She trusted this was all a part of his life plan. She rested in a profoundly deep love for her boy. While Almost-Young-Man's critical thinking deepened, there was Welly with open arms prepared to welcome him when it was time. I swear I saw her planning a welcome home party one morning as she S-Uh-shined in her sanctuary.

After years of traveling, shifting, and moving about the country, an almost two-year absence, Almost-Young-Man did return, with stories of New Zealand's sheep-speckled hillsides and fjords filled with water as black as midnight sky. When Almost-Young-Man did return, Welly ran through the house to retrieve her bunny toy. Perhaps she chose to showcase her bunny toy that had been added to her list of favorites while her boy was out in the world stretching, reaching, and growing. After all, Welly did have stories to share with him about the numerous times she prevented bunny predators from eating the garden delights. Although her mad searching in the house felt to me as if she was not ready to receive his arrival, truth was, her emotions were off the chart and her celebration looked like a dog with limited grasp of the English language. Dispersed emotions are one way our four-legged brothers and sisters express ecstatic bliss. The boy was home. Figuratively. Home. Welly knew he was here in this sanctuary moment and yet may not be in the next.

Home is right there, in the in-between. I watched my son go from boy to teen and now observed him slipping into his almost-young-man season. Nothing ever comes completely together in life. Things come together and fall apart, come together and fall apart. Relationships are solid, and then one abandons the other. We get connected to the team at work, and then the team dissolves until a new team is formed. The waters in the river are smooth, until they are not, until they are again. Waves come together, then crash, and then recede. The boy visits and leaves and visits again. I am an influential leader, then my old-fashioned ways no longer match the progression in the company, until the company's vision stalls. I am daughter, then an orphaned kid after parents' death, and then I am the parent who will orphan a child. I am girl, then woman, then woman seeking the girl inside of her.

Coming together and falling apart is the natural order of things. It is in this repetitive cycle of beginning and ending and beginning and ending again that the sacred space arises. This is the space of sanctuary where we can gather strawberries and cantaloupe and almonds and toss a salad for ourselves. It's the time to hum while washing the windows. It's time to care for our bodies and whisper-walk to humble ourselves. It's time to make amends, befriend our misgivings, and start anew.

Jesus came and then He left. Yet, it was in the sacred space between his walking on earth and his resurrection that the opportunity to be transformed as humans appeared. Grace came when we were open, present, and willing to consider the unfolding miracle that was occurring through His resurrected self years ago. Opportunity to be better and love bigger came in the in-between.

In the space of sanctuary, we aren't required to be the savior or the star. In sanctuary we are not on the battlefield or hurried or harried. In sanctuary, we are enough. We can empty our pockets of all the dimes we have been lugging around for decades, cosmic years, hundreds of seasons, and millennia ago and cash them in. We can abandon the dishtowels that stifle our creativity and bear down upon us to prevent us from becoming our evolved authentic beautiful selves.

In sanctuary space we find ourselves in between the breath out and the next breath in. Together influences the falling apart and the coming together. They are symbiotic events, and when I can see the pattern as part of my natural order of self-evolution, I can say goodbye, take some pig food, and all the feels that come from eating from the trough. Finally, I can move toward the mountain named Evolutionary Spirit.

When it all gets to be maybe a bit much, we can break its neck and grab a spot on the carpet for rug-readjustment. *There* is where the coming together and the falling apart meets, and there is where grace enters. In rug-adjustment time, traveling foreign lands, or in the bowl of strawberries, we can soak grace in. Sometimes, even sanctimonious grace comes in the breath of abandonment. Abandoning the old thinking and the old ways of being and operating. I know it is not comfortable to find myself with prairie dog breath or pig food on my lips. It's necessary. But, granting myself permission to be in the middle, to feel all the colossal emotions that come with being in that space, is essential in the chaos of life transition. In that space, grace cometh.

Noel came to be with my son and me in the space between the end of one season and the beginning of an end of a new season. The knock on the door came in sanctuary, and I didn't even recognize I was sitting right there in the middle of it. Snake blood, a son hiking in foreign lands, and scared bunnies running from threat is not pretty. But the longer I hang in there between the walking and the resurrection, the brighter the light gets and the more clarity I gain on that rug I sanctuary upon. The more equipped and prepared I become for the next.

Isaiah 60:1 (ISV)
Arise, shine! For your light has come.

Step #31

Exercise Your Authority

NOEL OFFERED ME A DAILY reminder of what life should and can be. Life changes, and the period of forced metamorphosis can feel chaotic. Yet in the shift, I required myself to unravel limited beliefs and uncover wounds that needed healing. Believing there was no room for me to recreate myself in my midlife season was limited thinking. Believing I had no time to transcend, to soar, to arise from lessons already learned so I may intentionally carry those into the next season was limited thinking. Believing days of me being a poet or speaker was limited thinking. Healing started to come from smiling at some of my past misgivings while choosing redemption. I broke the neck of those oozing sores. I forced myself to sit in the bed for three days after being gored by some truths I did not want to face. I began to consciously un-become so much of who I was in a different era. Thanks to Welly and her holy ways, I started to work to become what I needed to be to not only survive but thrive into my future. Noel offered a model and a safe space for the evolution of Teenager and middle-aged, angsty me. She graced a space that offered opportunity for a boy to walk his adolescent journey and a mom to somewhat gracefully and joyfully walk into a new chapter of life. Some days my evolution came painstakingly slow, while in others the lightbulb shown so bright—you know what's coming—I had to wear shades.

I gave myself permission. Permission was granted to feel the loss, the pride, the wonderment, the dirt upon my ankles as I stood in the rut. I accepted the changing colors hanging off my limbs in the season of Noel's visit. I invited her to provide the knowingness that can come while hibernating. I will shed, and I will emerge out of the winter's cold and fierce snow, a tree again, perhaps more weathered but stronger, more flexible in the winds and even more deeply rooted in that which I believe.

Noel's rock game served as a metaphor for the natural process of growth that includes patterns of reaching and returning. Reach and return. Stretch and retract. After following her calling to spread the Good News, Noel's reputation was stained in some circles, but her courage served as comfort to me when I had to say or do things in my professional world that felt somewhat up stream. Her rising to speak provided a palpable example of the power of using and valuing my own voice for empowerment. Her moments of S-Uh-shine so magically modeled the power of reflection, surrendering, rejuvenation, daydreaming, praying, repentance, and patience in waiting for the next miracle to arrive. Noel modeled what weaning looks like as I watched her allow her boy to leave so he may transform. So much of what Noel did was simply the natural order of things. Noel's play reminded me, if done well, we can stay the children we always were, even while our relationship with our self matures.

Noel, the dog of many names, taught all who entered her story. "Life is hard," she would say. "But we got this. We are equipped. We are capable of fighting our own giants because, in it all, He's got this." She was gifted with a drive of an unwavering commitment to protect while experiencing unabashed joy in each day. Noel never walked alone, although alone she found herself many times.

Noel taught me that, with a violent shake of a head, I can reorganize, recreate, and reinvent my hope, my vision, my behaviors, my thinking, and my ways! I can grab that tired story and break its neck. I can invite new light on this, my never-traveled path.

1 John 4:4 (ESV)
Little children, you are from God and have
overcome them, for he who is in you is
greater than he who is in the world

Quench Your Thirst at the Well

WELLY, THE DOG OF MANY names, lived a huge and colorful life. Geese, buck, bunnies, coyotes, and prairie dogs filled her daily agenda. But so too did the boy of a human mom who talked too much.

I am witness. Noel spent years communing with trees and chomping acorns with her few leftover side teeth. Seasons of rolling among grasses, sand, and newly fallen snow provided bliss. I got to witness her inspiring others with her agility, flexibility, and balance in all things called life.

After years of traveling and learning and falling and coming back together, Almost-Young-Man settled for a quick bit just a few miles away from me. I suppose those sugar-sweetened days of him being close enough to take Welly to his home for days at a time was the beginning of another coming together and the beginning of another falling apart. In hindsight, Almost-Young-Man arrived just in time.

Noel was suffering from a rare skin disease that devoured her flesh from the inside out. Wounds would appear on the sides of her ribs. Those wounds began to strip away the very framework of what made her *she*. Her caretaking was painstakingly arduous and included the wearing of T-shirts twenty-four hours a day. One day, as we were placing her Superman (with a capital S) T-shirt on her ravaged little body, she looked deep into our eyes and through mental telepathy demanded, "*We will never speak of these shirts.*"

So we didn't. And don't.

Occasionally, Almost-Young-Man would take her to his outdoor work site, and she would lay under the trees' shade while squinting her eyes with each gentle breeze. She S-Uh-shined while he worked, and when my son required a drink of water, he went to Ah-Well-Well. He gave her a pat, told her she was a good girl, promised he would care for her, and celebrated their coming home. With one-name Noel, the two quenched their thirst together at the well.

It was my turn to care for Noel in my home for a few days. This short season with her gave me time to recognize her leaves had fallen off, her sun had dimmed, and her determination to heed the call had waned. Soaked T-shirts and interrupted nights of panting and bleeding were a clear sign fall had come. Noel, the dog of many names, didn't seem inspired to take whatever was ravaging her from the inside out and break its neck.

And because this is a story about dimes and a boy-turned-man, an otherworldly presence, and light entering into a space that was feeling a little gloomy-ish, and snakes too, it is also about me. And Noel. Noel. Yes, Noel.

Psalm 23:4 (KJV)
Yea, though I walk through the valley of the shadow of death, I will fear no evil: for thou art with me; thy rod and thy staff they comfort me.

Step #33

Make Amends to Move Beyond

THE SUN ROSE, THE KNOWINGNESS entered every space and place in my home, in my walk, and in my life. Today, Noel would have the best day ever.

In her favorite portable bed, she was placed. With her in the backseat, we rolled the window down but did not turn on the radio. This was business, and we had a lot of ground to cover. We went to our favorite parks and carried her to the shadiest of trees. We visited grandparents in their outdoor gazebo and gave love pats among the birds' songs. We came home and soaked up the S-Uh-shine on Worn Rug. Steak was gobbled for dinner with an extra side of fat.

In the evening dusk, her bed was gingerly placed on the front porch, and the refreshingly cool breeze invited her to sit and absorb the day's ending. As I sat in the porch chair next to Welly, I watched her stand in a gingerly fashion and abandon her bed.

In the time it took me to shake my head back and forth a few times and break the neck of this surreal moment, she appeared again. In her mouth was her flattened bunny toy. They both crawled back into the safety of her porch bed.

I knew. I watched. I learned.

Noel was making amends, repenting, recovering, and receiving grace and forgiveness and love. She had spent months, I now realize, in the in-between. She had been practicing and knew it was time to prepare. She was considering to consider what the next season for her evolved self would be.

Philippians 3:10 (NIV)
...yes, to know the power of his resurrection...

Step #34

Cry on Sundays

SUNDAY ARRIVED GENTLY, HUMBLY, AND without fanfare. It arrived with the dawn of the day, as did the veterinarian. Almost-Man arrived with heavy shoulders, sodden feet, melted heart, and Friend that had been renamed Love in hand. Almost-Man joined his wiry-haired, once heart-shaped-faced sister and now child on the back deck, where she had hunted so many predators and kept watch for years. Noel saw him enter the space where she lay upon her bed placed just so. Bed and Noel, basking in the S-Uh-shine. Almost-Man approached her and lowered his body horizontally alongside hers so their two heads met and whispers could be exchanged. Noelly's mouth reached toward his ear and a kiss escaped. Within her kiss, I heard their intimate exchange deep within my being. Noel whisper-thought, "*You're my boy. I love you. You are enough. You are already perfect. I am with you.*"

The sun was intentional in its dance, and its rays pierced every pore of our bodies. The breeze caressed the very contours of our faces and gently brushed the back of our hands, like warm butter. Noelly lapped up chocolate ice cream and kissed her boy's wrists and calloused palms in gratitude. I watched Almost-Man caress her brow as if to make sure each hair within her heart-shaped countenance was perfectly placed.

It was there, in that very moment, of all time, in this universe, with all of us around her, she finally surrendered.

In the fog of unbearable grief, with chest held high, Man lifted the weight of Noel's limp body that lay upon her bed. Man picked her up as if she were a queen upon a throne. Presenting her to the Heavens, he stood strong and firm. I scarce could take it in. With tears streaming, he looked upon her, felt the absence of her earthly presence, and sadly, humbly, he honored Noel's resurrection.

On that day, I saw. Somewhere between teenaged hormones, soaring with his wings and returning home, in the silent space of sanctuary, he had grown, had found his own call.

In the space of the presence of snakes, grace, and divine dog, Man had found the sanctuary that offered sacred time to transcend him from boy to man. He had weaned himself. Not too far to forget where he came from, but far enough to move forward.

I too had weaned myself. I am free! From shrouds, coupons, snake nightmares, and melancholy grief. I was free from work ick after having been granted the new job I created. I cannot say I rid myself of snakes, Noel did that. Every last one. The miracle I had believed was coming came. She did indeed arrive. I can say, finally, I rid myself of snake stench and vial, dark, creepy thoughts. Somewhere in the not knowing how to rid my life of snakes, an otherworldly presence miraculously arrived and evicted each one of them. A dim turned to light in the silent space of sanctuary. I had grown and way-made a new and improved next season. I weathered and transformed in my own right. I weaned myself from the previous season just far enough to move forward yet not too far to forget where I came. On this day of Noelly's transcendence, we saw the parallel that occurred for Man, Noel, and me; the three of us in the same point in time, in the same universe, had concurrently worked to transcend into a new season.

In Mountain Peak's glory, the sun's rays, and the gentle valley breeze that danced among us after Noel's grand ascension, we gathered. We looked at one another.

We recalled Welly's final breath.

We fell apart.

1 Corinthians 13:11 (NIV)
When I was a child, I talked like a child, I
thought like a child, I reasoned like a child.
When I became a man, I gave up childish ways.

Step #35

Return to Step #1 When It's Time. and You WILL Know When It's Time

NOEL MET JESUS WITHOUT HER teeth.

She lives in the tumultuous waters and the crunch of acorns. She lives in the memory and ties the ancestral lineage even tighter. She lives among the trees and the squirrels and the prairie dogs. And yes, the snakes too. She lives with the bear, the coyotes, and the deer. She still competes for her fastest time on each path I walk. She lives in Man's heart and she lives in mine.

One time, Jesus came to way make while inspiring a dog, a teen, and a woman in the midst of their snake-infested life-season transition. These now told stories were about dimes and a boy-turned-man, an otherworldly presence, and light entering into a space that was feeling a little gloomy-ish, and snakes too. But, mostly, this was a story about Noel. N-o-e-l. Yes, Noel.

Today, I can confidently claim, *both* Jesus and Noel are transformed. They have transcended and ascended. Now, even Ah-Well-Well lives again. With us. In new form.

He lives and so does "he." Yes, Jesus lives and so does "he," the dog who was once called "he."

And so do I, in my next life season.

Now. This is the time. This is where I turn up the volume, close my eyes, let the tears flow and belt out Alan Jackson's hymn, "He Lives."

About the Author

Staci McCormack is a woman of many hats, each reflecting a different layer of her rich, vibrant journey. A *member of Earth, child of the Universe, and daughter of God,* Staci is grounded in her connection to both the divine and the natural world. Raised by wise and humble ancestors, she has evolved through seasons, storms, and sunlight into a resilient truth seeker who finds peace, love, joy, and purpose within.

With a career spanning over three decades, Staci has worn a multitude of professional roles—waitress, teacher, school principal, burger flipper, executive, preacher's kid, freelance writer, and, ultimately, a nationally trained retreat leader. Throughout these varied experiences, she has always returned to the core belief that the answers we seek are found not only within ourselves but in the heart of nature and in the Trinity.

Staci is the proud facilitator of Sacred Walk, where she leads transformative retreats and workshops. Her work spans across communities of women and organizations, helping others create spaces of calm and connection amidst life's challenges. She spent 30 years in education, including spearheading efforts in Colorado to foster connectedness and positive school cultures that work to prevent bullying, isolation and suicide ideation. Her expertise in fostering a sense of calm in the midst of adversity is invaluable, as is her ability to work with those in life transition.

Despite her professional success, Staci never loses sight of her personal life. She is a mother, a best friend, neighbor, sister, partner, Christian, pet-sitter, hippie, and dreamer. She is also known for her playful, silly spirit—always a joy to be around.

Today, Staci continues her evolution, embracing new paths and new possibilities. As she writes, serves, and nurtures her own growth—attending to her chakras, healing, stretching, and exploring—she is fully committed to becoming the person God created her to be in each season of life.

Her journey is far from over, and as she continues to walk her Sacred Walk, she invites others to join her on the path of self-discovery, evolution, healing, and connection.

www.ingramcontent.com/pod-product-compliance
Lightning Source LLC
Chambersburg PA
CBHW021105130626
46554CB00002B/543